SHTF DISASTER SURVIVAL GEAR GUIDE A TO Z

BEST BUG OUT GEAR & SUPPLY MANUAL

By

Robbie J. Jones

Henry Miller

Published by:

CSB Academy Publishing Company.
P.O. Box 966
Semmes, Alabama 36575

Cover & Interior designed

By

Angie Anderson

First Edition

CONTENTS AT A GLANCE

FOREWORD

AS I MENTIONED in "Ultimate Disaster Prep & Planning Handbook" the world has been changing at a faster pace than ever before. No one knows what tomorrow will bring. But if you are like me, then you most likely would agree that just waiting for something to happen is not something I want to do. Instead, I want to be ready and prepared in case a disaster happens.

Just look through last 20 years headlines, the world has seen more terrorist attacks, civil unrest, large scale riots, looting, nuclear threats, active shooter situations, major wars and school shootings than ever before. If you think this the new normal of the 21st century, let me be the first to disagree with you strongly. These are not, but this is a new reality. We have to learn to accept it, and I have, but as the world is changing, I have decided to change a little too.

What if there is an attack in your city or mine? Will we be prepared? As a professional hiker, I have traveled the world for years. I have met many interesting people along the way. But one group of people that stood out from all the rest were five guys I met in Columbia. I was their hiking coach for a week, and we were off to a very rough terrain when one of them asked me if I could teach them about disaster preparation and wilderness survival. I was surprised to hear his question, but the concerned look on his face told me he was dead serious. That question opened my mind and eyes wide open, and I realized I was not alone, there are people who fear the same as I do.

When I taught disaster survival courses, I always told people, SHTF preparation is not all about just stockpiling food, water and securing a shelter. Well think about it, if you only need to take shelter and hide for a week, yes, then it is fine to just have food, water, and a secure shelter.

But what if the disaster is truly a big and longer lasting one? Would be okay with just those three items? Or would you need to have a few more things to survive for the long run? Ideally, disaster preparation is much more than just that; a true preparation would be where you learn a few basic survival skills, master them, practice them and become a pro at them. To be truly successful, you need to take a comprehensive approach and look at the broader picture, and that is exactly what I have done in these three books.

A true survivor is a person who knows how to survive in any situation and make the best out of it. A true survivor knows how to find food, water, or shelter when there is none. A true survivor knows how to deal with any emergencies when there is no 911 service to call.

Any book on this topic can show you how and what food to stockpile, but is that is just a small part of survival training, a big part of that training is where you learn what skills you will need, how to learn and master such skills, what gears and supplies you need, what to use, how to use them. This book is all about preparation and what gears to use and how to use them properly.

Let's get started...

TYPES OF SURVIVAL BAGS

IF YOU READ the first book in this series, you should now be aware of the many events that can completely change the world around you. Depending on the event, you can have days, hours, minutes or something only seconds to react. Over time, those who are focused on preparing for disasters have come up with a number of bags or kits that anyone would need to deal with any emergency.

Each bag or kit has a basic outline of items to include and from there each can be customized to meet individual or family needs as well as events specific to your location. Let's look at each type of bag, so you know what you need to prepare for.

EVERY DAY CARRY (EDC)

PURPOSE

The main reason for an EDC kit is to keep your prepared at any moment for unexpected events. It will provide the supplies needed to defend and protect you and your family in the event you can't get to any of your other stockpiled supplies. The EDC is supposed to be lightweight, discreet and something you carry with you at all times.

HOW TO CARRY/STORE

An EDC kit is supposed to be carried on you at all time, not in a bag or backpack instead you can carry it in a pocket, clip it to your belt, attach it to a key ring, place it in your wallet or purse or an ankle holster.

WHAT'S INCLUDED

The contents of an EDC kit need to be customized to your specific location and any potential situations you may encounter, but it also needs to meet your skill level. A gun won't do you any good unless you know how to use it properly. Later in this book we are going to take a look at each bag or kit in detail, so we'll have a longer list of the items to include there. The smallest form of this kit can include a detail disaster plan along with some cash and a multipurpose knife of some sort.

CAR BUG OUT BAG (CAR BOB)

PURPOSE

These BOB bags are designed specifically for your car so you can be prepared for any type of emergency that occurs when you are out driving your car. These kits not only include car maintenance and repairs, but also some survival gear for natural disasters and other similar emergencies.

HOW TO CARRY/STORE

You obviously want to keep this kit in your car at all times. Most people place all the items in a duffel bag that they keep in the trunk. However, depending on your vehicle and the items you're carrying you can also store it in the rear cargo area, glove compartment, front center console, driver or passenger door, under each seat, seat back mesh pockets, a rooftop storage rack or a rear rack.

GET HOME BAG (GHB)

PURPOSE

The GHB is a kit designed to get you from Point A to your home and should be kept within easy reach. Generally, these packs are only designed for short trips of several hours up to 24 hours should you be delayed. These kits are designed for any disaster, or emergency that occurs while you are away from home.

HOW TO CARRY/STORE

The GHB is for items you need to get home after an emergency or disaster situation, but are too bulky to include in an EDC. The GHB is another customized kit. Since you will be carrying the kit with you, it should be discreet and able to blend into most settings.

BUG OUT BAG (BOB)

PURPOSE

This is the big one. This is the bag designed to hold everything you and your family needs to survive at least 72 hours or even up to one week away from your home. This bag is kept at home with easy access so you can grab it quickly when you need to evacuate and go to a pre-determined bug out location. The BOB is your lifeline if you ever need to evacuate your home.

I'M NEVER COMING HOME (INCH)

PURPOSE

This bag is exactly what it sounds like. You use this bag whenever you know for sure or are pretty sure you are never going to be able to return to your home after evacuation. This is the most comprehensive bag you can pack for survival, and it isn't going to be the type you can carry on your back.

WHEN TO CARRY/STORE

This bag is often kept at home, garage or other secure location. It is often a fully-packed bag that needs to be transported in a vehicle to your new destination. The INCH bag often contains what you need to create a new home and sustain you and your family for several months or longer.

PET BUG OUT BAG (PET BOB)

PURPOSE

This bag is designed for those who have pets and need to provide for them for whatever period the emergency or disaster situation is going to last or until you can get to a more stable location.

HOW TO CARRY/STORE

Ideally, your pet will be able to carry their own BOB; especially for larger domestic animals. Otherwise, is should be a part of your BOB or INCH bag.

As you can tell, there are a lot of survival kits and even more survival gear that goes into them. It can often be an overwhelming challenge for the new preparer to determine what goes into these bags. In this book, I'm going to show you just how to prepare each of these bags and how to choose the right equipment that goes into them. But first, let's answer the most common question of all.

DIY VS. PREMADE SURVIVAL BAGS/KITS

When it comes to survival bags and kits, the biggest question many people ask is whether they should put the kit together themselves or just buy one that is premade. I'm a fan of making your own, and I'll give you several reasons why I feel it is a bad idea to buy premade survival kits.

COST

One would think that buying a premade kit would be cheaper. In fact, these kits can sometimes be as much as $600. On the other hand, you can often put together your own kit for less than $300. It all depends on your customized needs and how much time you have to put into shopping for the gear that goes into your bag. For just the basics it is possible to put together a kit for under $100 if you shop and buy right.

CUSTOMIZATION

A premade bag is going to give you a little bit of everything. They are basically one-size fits all solution but don't consider any individual needs a buyer may have. There are many factors that influence what you put into a kit including the following:

➢ Age

➢ Sex

➢ Location

➢ Climate

➢ Medical conditions

- ➤ Bug out location

- ➤ Type of disasters

However, when selling a premade bag they have to cast a wide net to attract customers. Even if you do buy a premade bag, you are going to have to invest some extra money to include missing essentials that you are going to need after customization.

NO ROOM FOR EXTRAS

Manufacturers of premade kits want to keep things lightweight and compact, so you won't find much empty room inside. So it will be difficult for you add additional items to these bags. Instead, it's best to get your own empty bag and add your own gear since it will save you time, money and frustration.

LEARNING TO USE THE GEAR

When you buy a premade kit you typically just toss it in a closet and forget about it until you actually need it. When you put together a kit on your own, you will be able to learn about items and how to use them.

Before choosing an item that goes into your kit, you should research several brands and read the specs of each to see which one suits your needs better. You'll be reading reviews from others who've used the product and learn the pros and cons. You open the packaging and get to actually hold the item which helps you to get used to the item. Then you can take the step of actually testing the gear, something a lot of people don't take the time to do.

ROTATION

Those who buy premade packs often forget the important fact that you have to rotate your stockpile on occasion. Food spoils, especially when stored someplace warm like a closet. It is best to rotate your stock at least twice a year during daylight savings time. This will ensure your bug out bags are always fresh, usable and ready for use.

NO TOOLS FOR FOOD AND WATER

Often the target audiences for a premade bag are those who haven't developed any important survival skills. They may not know how to start a fire, purify water or source their own food. A premade bag is designed to help you survive for 72 hours, but after that, the bag won't help you find food, water, and shelter.

Now let's take a quick look at a few of the pros you get from a premade BOB so you can consider both points:

➢ Convenience - You don't need a lot of time or effort to put it together.

➢ Expertise - The creators of the bags generally have done some research about the supplies they put into their bags.

➢ Basics are Covered - Most premade bags will at least give you adequate basic coverage for 72 hours; which is a good starting point.

If you absolutely feel you need to get a premade BOB for some reason then at least consider the following when choosing which one to purchase.

CHOOSING A PREMADE BOB

➢ Are the essentials covered?

➢ How many additional items do you need to add?

➢ Are the contents something you need or are you getting useless items?

➢ Is the kit for your home or car?

➢ Will you be able to carry it for long distances?

➢ Will it cover all the people in your group?

When you ask these questions, you will at least be able to get a decent premade BOB. However, I still say you should build your own. And with that in mind let's start looking at what you need to know.

BUG OUT BAG (BOB)

NO MATTER how much planning you put into the contents of your BOB, you won't get very far unless you choose the right bag for your supplies. A great BOB needs to be compact, yet big enough to hold all the supplies you need. It has to be a lightweight, sturdy and recognizable as your BOB without being so flashy that it draws attention.

How to do you know what BOB bag is best for you? There are some important elements you need to consider and choosing the right one is the most important first step. First, let us consider what type of BOB bag is best for you.

TYPES OF BOBS

BACKPACK

This can include a range of bags since it can be anything from a school book bag to a tactical assault type bag. There is a wide range of options in this category and it is the most commonly chosen for a BOB since it offers a good balance between size and variety. It is best for one to two people or if you are bugging out in a group where everyone carries their own supplies.

DUFFEL BAG

These often have more volume than a backpack, but can be a little difficult to carry. However, these are a good option if you are going to be bugging out in a vehicle and already have a second destination in mind. Just keep in mind you don't want to carry this type of bag on your back over uneven ground for an extended period of time.

HIKING PACK

This option gives you the best features of both a backpack and duffel bag. It offers you a large volume and ergonomic carrying options. You can carry more survival gear in one of these compared to a backpack, which makes it a great option if you are evacuating with a family.

BOB FACTORS TO CONSIDER

COMFORT AND FIT

Keep in mind you may be hiking with your BOB for days. Therefore, you need something that you can comfortably wear without limiting your movement or causing discomfort. When looking at the comfort and fit of a BOB, look for the following:

Hip Straps and Hip Padding

When looking for a BOB with good comfort and fit are two most important things to look for. Hip support straps help hold the pack tightly to your hip so the weight can be carried by the strong muscles in your thighs and hips rather than leaving the load to your shoulders. This also helps with balance by lowering the center of gravity and taking the weight off your back and shoulders. This makes it much easier to carry a heavy load.

Width of Straps

Make sure the straps aren't made of narrow webbing that will dig into your shoulders and hips. Rather you want straps that are wide with plenty of padding to cushion where it attaches to your body.

Sternum Clip

This allows you to secure the shoulder straps in a comfortable position and uses the bony part of your chest to counterbalance any backward leaning as a result of the weight of the BOB.

Airflow on the Back

If your back sweats and you walk all day, chafing and discomfort can result. Good BOB has channels or webbing in part of the pack that is touching your back. This allows the air to flow through which reduces sweating and discomfort.

Hard Elements Inside the Pack

These elements will rub or poke into you. Some bags have a rigid frame or hard plastic pieces that help them to maintain their shape or allow you to strap things to them. You don't need to avoid these bags as a whole, but it is something to consider when choosing a BOB.

Gender Specific Designs

Most bags come in the both male and female options. The straps are cut and shaped in different ways to better fit the designated gender.

WEIGHT AND COMFORT

This is one of the biggest factors to consider. Remember that you are going to be carrying the pack for three days or more and traveling a lot of miles. This means you need to choose a lightweight bag that is still durable and comfortable when fully loaded.

A great style is an internal frame backpacking bag. These work for hiking and camping so they are designed to be lightweight while also being sturdy and comfortable. The only negative to these packs are their cost. Often you will spend about $150 for a decent internal frame backpack.

STORAGE CAPACITY

Next on the list of things to consider is the storage capacity of your BOB. You are going to need to fit three or more days of survival gear, so your average daypack isn't enough. The main compartment of the bag is important for holding the majority of your supplies. The main compartment should be big enough for clothes, large food items and possibly even weapons.

In addition to space within the large central compartment, you also need to consider other pockets and attachment points on the bag. The more zippered and strapped pockets the bag has the better it is. More pockets mean you can be more organized, which is the key in a survival situation.

The last thing to consider is the attachment points. Since you're likely going to need to bring a sleeping bag, a bed roll, and some tarp; you'll want these to easily attach to the outside of your pack. You don't want to place these inside the bag itself as they could get the interior wet and dirty.

ACCESSIBILITY

If you have a big list of survival equipment, putting everything in a single large compartment can be challenging and frustrating. You never want to dig for something you need under some other items you don't need.

What you want for efficiency is a bag that has one large compartment to store your general items and several smaller, separate compartments where you can store smaller subgroups of items. Most modern bags have multiple compartments and/or the option to attach smaller satellite bags. This will make finding things easier in a hurry.

Once you have chosen a bag that meets your basic needs, you can determine if there are some advanced features you want or need.

Hydration Bladder Compatibility

The integration of a hydration system is a major bonus to a BOB. This makes it easier to carry large amounts of water. Since you will be exerting yourself, you are going to need to keep properly hydrated.

Rain Hood

Some modern bags come with a rain cover integrated into it. This is often tucked away into a Velcro compartment and pulled out and over the bag when needed. This is a good option to keep your gear dry.

MOLLE Compatibility

This is an acronym for Modular Lightweight Load-carrying Equipment. It is a current generation of load-bearing equipment and packs that some armed forces use. This means you can find some compatible options when adding accessories to a MOLLE compatible bag. Some items include tool sheaths, pouches, hydration bladders and medical kits.

As with other aspects of disaster preparation, the last thing you want to do is attract attention to yourself and your gear. The more you can blend in with everyone else, the better off you will be.

There are two ways your bag could stand out that you want to avoid. First, you don't want it to look too much like a military bag. Second, you want to avoid bright colors or wild patterns that make it very noticeable. It is best to stick with neutral colors such as light brown or khaki.

INTERNAL FRAMES VS. EXTERNAL FRAMES

For you BOB you will have to decide between light vs. heavy and internal vs. external frames. Internal frames have a hidden frame inside the pack. These can't hold as much weight, but they are more flexible and position most of the weight on your hips rather than your shoulders. These are most suitable for a standard three day BOB and allow for faster movement.

External frame packs are stronger and heavier. As the name suggests the pack is supported by a visible frame. These packs are almost always larger, meaning they can handle more heavy duty gear such as tents, tarps and even bed rolls. If you want a heavier BOB that will last longer than a week, the external frame is a good choice.

DETERMINE HOW YOU'LL USE YOUR PACK

Before you buy a BOB or backpack, you first want to consider what situations your BOB is for and any special circumstances you might be faced with.

HOW LONG DO YOU NEED IT FOR?

Obviously, you want your BOB to be big enough to hold all the items you need for a specific amount of time. A good rule of thumb is to make sure your BOB has enough room for gear to keep you alive for at least three days or 72 hours. A great BOB, however, will have enough supplies that can stretch you to five or six days of survival.

WHAT TYPE OF ENVIRONMENT WILL YOU USE IT IN?

The location you will be traveling in also has a heavy influence on what you pack in your BOB. For example, if you live in colder regions you are going to need to pack extra sets of warm clothing, fire starting materials and shelter building items. Your BOB needs to keep you safe no matter what situation you find yourself in during an emergency.

In addition to weather and climate, you also want to consider geography and terrain. If you are near a river or lake, you should consider packing a complete fishing kit. It would also be a good idea to waterproof everything.

Before starting on your BOB, you need to consider what specific kind of emergencies or disasters are most likely to occur in your area. You wouldn't want to pack for an emergency that isn't likely to occur in your area.

CONSIDER YOUR HEALTH

This is often one of the most overlooked aspects of choosing and preparing a BOB. If you or anyone in your family has specific health conditions, then you should certainly take this into account.

If you aren't in good shape, then you should consider building a lighter BOB. A heavier pack would slow you down and/or cause you to over exert yourself. If a family member can't walk well for a long distance, then you'll need to include special items to assist them, carry them or provide adequate rest breaks.

If your health conditions require medications, you should also include plenty of medications in your BOB as well. Sometimes medicines end up being more important than having a weapon.

TEST IT

The last step in choosing a good BOB is to test it. Pack it with what you need and take it for a hike. How far can you go without getting tired? Is anything poking you or making you uncomfortable?

Often a bag may feel fine when you first start hiking, but it may start bothering you after a few miles.

Along with packing and hiking with your BOB to test it, you should also practice packing and unpacking it to make sure things are packed in the right order. There are many ways to pack your BOB, and some can be better than others. If the bag doesn't work for your specific needs, then return it for another bag. Don't keep anything that doesn't work perfectly for you.

There are a number of packs that will meet the criteria we've set out above, but it all comes down to your personal preference. This is an important first step in your disaster preparedness, and it will make a great improvement on bugging out when an event occurs. Next, let's take a look at the essentials you need to pack in your BOB.

BOB ESSENTIAL GEAR

The general rule of thumb is that a well designed BOB should weight no more than 30% of your body weight. Any more weight than this will be highly strenuous and limit your ability to hike over a long distance which might be required in a survival situation. This means you are likely going to want to limit your BOB gear to the bare essentials or items that have a high chance of allowing you to survive a disaster situation.

The purpose of this segment is just to give you the list of BOB essential gear. There is much more and no limit as to what you can put into your kit based on your needs. So here it is:

Survival Essentials:

✓ Batteries

✓ Camping Hammock

✓ Can Opener

✓ Dry Bag

✓ Duct Tape

✓ Emergency Blanket

✓ Emergency Radio

✓ Fire Starters

✓ First Aid Kit

✓ Flashlight

✓ Headlamp

✓ Hydration Bladder

✓ Map and Compass

✓ Multi-Tool

✓ Paracord

- ✓ Pocket Knife
- ✓ Poncho
- ✓ Rations
- ✓ Signal Mirror
- ✓ Sleeping Bag
- ✓ Spare Clothes
- ✓ Survival Whistle
- ✓ Tarp
- ✓ Tent
- ✓ Tomahawk
- ✓ At least a gallon of water

Sanitation Items:

- ✓ Bug Repellent
- ✓ Hygiene Kit
- ✓ Water Filtering Item
- ✓ Water Purification Tablets
- ✓ Wet Towelettes

Urban Survival Items:

- ✓ Dust Mask
- ✓ Pry Tool
- ✓ Hydrant / Gas Main Tool
- ✓ Work Gloves

Wilderness Survival Items:

- ✓ Camp Shovel
- ✓ Camping Saw
- ✓ Hatchet
- ✓ Survival Knife
- ✓ Filet Knife
- ✓ Hunting / Skinning Knife

Hunting / Self Defense Items:

- ✓ Handgun
- ✓ Rifle
- ✓ Extra Ammunition
- ✓ Slingshot & Ammo
- ✓ Pepper Spray
- ✓ Fishing Kit

However, this is just a starting point. What you pack will depend on your unique situation. Consider what you are likely to need so you can make your own essentials list. Next, is the important aspect of organizing and packing your BOB.

BOB ORGANIZING AND PACKING

You will notice that your essential BOB items will fit into seven categories:

1. Shelter and safety or protection

2. Water

3. Fire starting

4. First aid

5. Hygiene

6. Food

7. Tools

The specific items you choose for each of the seven categories will depend on your unique personal situation. However, the most important thing you can have is knowledge. The more you know, the more useful the items in your BOB become in an emergency situation and less gear you'll have to carry.

When it comes to packing your BOB, the key is mobility with utility a close second. You cannot pack your BOB haphazardly and needs to be approached with a methodical process just like when you plan your BOB.

Just remember that the purpose of a BOB isn't to go hiking or take a camping trip, but to save a life in an emergency situation. Therefore, packing your survival kit and prioritizing items will be slightly different than it is from a hiking or camping trip. Although you'll still have to follow the rules of properly distributing your load.

When you properly pack your BOB, it will be easier to carry, and it will also carry more supplies. In general, it is best to keep heavy items lower in the bag and close to your back. The lighter items are the opposite.

Next, you need to organize your items into three categories:

1. Non-urgent

2. Urgent

3. Emergency

Non-urgent items are what go into your pack first and are items that won't be retrieved with any urgency. Non-urgent items would include the following:

> Extra clothing

> Bedding

> Hygiene

> Miscellaneous supplies

Urgent items are packed second for easier access and will include items like the following:

> Shelter

> Water

> Food

> Fire starters

Emergency items are those that need to be accessed at a moment's notice and should be kept on your person or within easy reach in the pockets of your pack. This would include items such as the following:

> Communication equipment

> Self-defense gear

> Flashlights

> Personal tools such as a survival knife

> Foul weather gear

Within each of these three categories, you need to compartmentalize items based on a system that makes sense to you so you can find things easily when you're in a hurry. As you pack your items, look for creative ways that you can save space. For example, wrap duct tape around a water bottle or pack items inside other items such as cooking pots.

You also want to remember to keep your gear dry. You can waterproof your items or use professional grade plastic bags or simple Ziploc bags. The main thing is to make sure your items are protected. You might also want to line your pack with an industrial strength garbage bag to add an extra layer of protection.

Now that you have your gear organized and packaged you can just store your BOB and forget it, right? Wrong. You are going to need to update your BOB at certain times every year.

BOB UPDATING

For most people, they stop their survival planning once they have a BOB packed and a bug out plan in place. This can be a major mistake with potentially fatal consequences. You may have your BOB sitting in your home for years before you actually need to use it. Then when a disaster strikes and you need to put your bug out plan in effect, you run out of your home only to find all your food has expired, or that your flashlight batteries are dead. Managing your disaster plan and BOB contents should be an ongoing process with refinements and adjustments made to both as you develop your survival preparedness.

It is best to review your BOB contents and emergency plan every quarter. At a minimum, you will need to check the basic elements.

FOOD EXPIRATION

Some survival rations can be safe up to five years, but many will spoil before then. You should make sure you check the shelf life on any food items that you rely on each quarter and replace anything before they go bad.

MEDICATIONS

Medications have a range of expiration dates. If you have any medications packed in your BOB such as antibiotics, insulin, EpiPens, heart medications or any others, then you need to know how long each is good for and replace as needed.

FIRST AID ITEMS

There are a lot of single use first aid items such as creams, antiseptic wipes, bandages and eyewash/irrigation solutions that have a limited shelf life. This expiration typically involves the sterility of an item, and when they become out of date, they shouldn't be used to treat injuries. You should conduct regular first aid kit inspections and replace any out of date items as needed.

ELECTRONIC BATTERIES

The best thing about having solar or hand cranked electronic items like a radio or flashlight is that you don't need to worry about batteries dying at a crucial moment. However, if you do have an item in your BOB that requires batteries, then you need to check them quarterly at a minimum to make sure they have enough charge to power your equipment.

An added preventative is to store electronic items with the two positive ends of two batteries facing each other, so the batteries don't drain. You could also keep the batteries stored outside of the electronics if you aren't going to use them for an extended time to avoid corrosion.

AMMUNITION

If you have a firearm and ammunition as a part of your BOB, then you should plan to test fire a few rounds at a minimum twice a year. If you have any misfires, you will need to replace the rounds from the batch with new ones.

OTHER TIMES TO UPDATE YOUR BOB

In addition to the above quarterly checks, you should also review both your survival gear and emergency plan any time your personal situation changes.

WHEN YOU MOVE

Moving can have major effects on your emergency plan. If you move from a rural area to an urban area or vice versa, then you are going to need to modify your BOB. If you changed climates, you'd need to update what spare clothes you keep in your BOB. You get the idea. Just remember to keep tailoring your BOB and survival gear to your specific situation.

CHANGES IN BUG OUT MEMBERS

If the members of your bug out group changes such as the addition of a family member or the departure of a family member then you are going to need to rethink your survival gear and change your plan as needed. If you add a member that needs special resources or someone with new skills, then you are going to need to adjust your plan and gear accordingly. Also, if you lose someone with a specific skill, you may need to get new gear to account for the loss of skill.

NEW THREATS

The modern world is constantly changing, and the status of external threats around you will change often. If a new threat arrives or if an old one increases in probability, you are going to need to update your BOB and emergency plan accordingly. For example, severe weather patterns or potentially new hazardous industrial facilities in the area.

Keep in mind that your BOB and emergency plan are constantly changing as new factors and information come along. There are many things that can affect your survival situation, and when you keep your BOB up to date, you will increase your chances of survival if a disaster happens. Many preparers will suggest that you set a reminder in a calendar on your phone to review your BOB contents at least quarterly. Before we start looking at the other bags, we should consider a few alternatives to the BOB.

SPECIAL ALTERNATIVES TO BOBS

A BOB is going to have essential and general survival gear. As we've stated before, you are going to customize the equipment you pack based on your specific needs and the situations you may face. However, there are also a few specific situations where you may need to consider a slightly modified version of a BOB.

WILDERNESS BOB

One thing you often hear when it comes to disaster preparedness is that each scenario has its own set of factors and challenges that influence how you determine your BOB contents.

PLANNING FACTORS

If you live in or are bugging out to a rural location, this presents you with both advantages and challenges. These will require some modifications to your BOB to make it a wilderness survival kit. These additional factors include the following:

❖ Increased chance of running into wild animals that are dangerous and/or poisonous.

❖ Lower population density means less potential for hostiles and fewer people to get assistance from.

- ❖ Smaller communities mean fewer options for scavenging survival supplies from abandoned locations.

- ❖ More opportunities to scavenge plants and hunt or trap game.

Survival Fishing Kit - If you are going to be near a body of water that has fish, you will be able to pack less food and instead catch your own fish if you have the skill. This allows you to either carry more survival supplies or travel lighter. A survival fishing kit is small enough to fit in your pocket and give you all the essentials you need.

Compass - Landmarks are harder to find and use for navigation in the wilderness. A compass and local map are essentials in a wilderness survival kit. Make sure you take a survival course in compass use and map reading.

Slingshot - This is light, easy to carry and can help you hunt small game if you don't have a weapon or the ability to set a snare.

Travel Hammock - This will save you time and energy on building a shelter every night. However, in colder weather, you are also going to need to add a sleeping bag.

Bug Repellent - This isn't necessarily a survival item, but avoiding annoying insects does improve morale and is a good idea to have on hand. While most people use a DEET-based bug spray, for a survival situation it can be better to use a Permethrin based repellent. Permethrin can be sprayed on clothes and gear, plus will last up to six washes. So if you have to swim a river or get caught in the rain, you won't need to reapply.

Pocket Guide to Local Plants - You should make sure this covers both edibles and poisonous plants, so you know what to eat and what to avoid. If possible get a guide that is focused specifically on your location.

Camping Shovel - You can use this to bury waste and garbage to keep animals away from your camp. It can also be used to build a shelter and as an improvised weapon should that be needed. A tri-fold shovel is your best option since it will take up the least amount of space in your BOB.

Filleting / Skinning Knife - You should choose one based on the type of animals that are caught and hunted in your local area. These tools will allow you to maximize the yield of your protein.

Hatchet - This is a valuable tool that can make a shelter and chop firewood.

Paracord - This goes along with the hatchet in terms of essential gear. Paracord is lightweight and compact, but extremely strong. You should have at least a hundred feet of paracord in your wilderness survival kit to build your shelter, make a rope ladder or tie a splint on a fracture.

Bear Spray - If you are going to be bugging out in a location known for bears then this is definitely something you want to pack with you.

These items can be added as needed to your BOB to customize it into a wilderness survival kit. Consider the environment around you to determine what works best for you. The more planning you do before a disaster means you will be better able to improvise and survive when a disaster strikes. On the other hand, if you live in an urban area you are going to need different items in your BOB.

URBAN BOB

PLANNING FACTORS

There are a number of unique factors to consider when bugging out in an urban environment. Be sure to consider the following when planning what items to pack in an urban BOB.

❖ Building debris and glass after a disaster.

❖ Increased chance to scavenge food and water from abandoned locations.

❖ The possibility of finding supply caches.

❖ Increased risk of encountering humans can be both a positive and a negative depending on the disposition of the individual and how you handle the situation.

❖ Decreased need for shelter since there will be a lot of buildings around.

URBAN SURVIVAL GEAR ESSENTIALS

Crow / Pry Bar - This can help with scavenging, removing barriers, clearing debris and hammering out the glass. You should choose a small variety that can easily fit in your BOB.

Tools for Fire Hydrants / Gas Mains - This is useful if you find a house with leaking gas or if you need to access a fire hydrant for clean water.

Multi-Tool - This gives you the versatility to perform different types of jobs, solve minor problems and take up minimal room in your BOB.

Work Gloves - If you have to break glass or move debris then these can save your hands.

Dust Mask - This will protect your lungs from any airborne debris particles after a building collapse.

Can Opener - There are going to be more options for scavenging food in an urban location than a rural one. A can opener allows you to easily access any food you come across.

In urban survival, you need to be prepared for the fact that you may encounter unfriendly people. Ideally, you will want to talk your way out of an encounter or avoid them entirely. However, this may not always be an option. If a fight does occur and you need to defend yourself then consider having a weapon on hand to protect yourself. We'll talk about weapons in a later chapter.

When you add the above items to your BOB, you will have an effective urban survival kit. Just make sure you ask yourself the following questions first:

✧ Do you want to pack non-perishable food for bugging out?

✧ Are you in an environment where you can use scavenger as you go?

✧ Are there factors that make the urban environment unique where you live?

✧ How do you plan to deal with other humans?

Another specialized BOB you need to consider is what you have to pack if you are bugging out with a family.

If you are a parent or you have a family with children in your bug out group, then there are a few important factors to consider when preparing your BOB and making your emergency plan compatible with the limitations of children in your group.

A family BOB differs from a standard BOB in a few major ways. While it still serves the same purpose, it also needs to be tailored to the needs of individuals with a wide range of skill sets and ages. Let's take a look at what you need to add based on each age group of children.

INFANTS AND TODDLES AGE 0-5

Combination Child Carrier and Pack - This will allow you to carry both your child and all your survival gear. Everything can be carried comfortably, and you will be able to cover more distance faster.

Diapers - This is obvious for parents, but is often overlooked when packing other survival gear. Reusable diapers are likely the best option. In addition, they can be multi-use and multipurpose because they can be used for other tasks in addition to their primary use.

Medicine Syringe / Eyedropper - This should be kept with any medication you're giving a child. You never want to improvise a medication delivery method. Medicine syringes are lightweight and don't require much room.

Formula - For an adult, you can pack rations or forage and hunt for food, but not with an infant or toddler. Even if a mother is still breastfeeding, you will do well to pack formula. This way another individual can feed the child if the mother isn't able to do so.

Pacifier - If your child needs a pacifier, have an extra one packed so you can be sure it comes with you. These will often help your child sleep and can help keep them quiet if you need to keep things low.

Extra Clothing - A general rule of thumb is to pack your family BOB with two more sets of clothing for your child than you would pack for an adult. This allows you to regulate their temperature by using layered clothing and also gives you options should there be a diaper accident.

Waterproof Bodysuit - This is important if you potentially encounter foul weather with an infant or toddler. It will help to keep them warm and dry; which also reduces your stress and keeps morale high.

Pre-Sterile Bottles - These are bottles that are sold in sterile packaging. It prevents you from needing to boil a bottle when feeding your child while evacuating. Be sure to monitor the expiration dates on any sterile items during your BOB reviews.

Sterilization Agent - You often find this in a concentrated powder or liquid that you dilute with water. If you need to use a bottle multiple times, you are going to eventually need to sterilize them. A few drops of the sterilizing agent mixed with water in a wide mouthed water bottle can be used to sterilize bottles or small objects.

BUG OUT PLANNING FOR INFANTS AND TODDLERS

For this age, it is important that you remember you are going to be carrying your child for the majority of the time you are bugging out after a disaster. In addition to the physical limitations of toddlers and infants; they are also emotionally and mentally traumatized by the disaster and the new surroundings.

This will often make the child needier and in constant contact with a parent. Since you are already going to be carrying the BOB, you also need to account for the weight of the child into your emergency plan. It will slow you down, and you are going to burn more calories. Plan your energy intake and rest stops based on this.

Noise reduction is also an important part of operational security. Most young children yell or cry to bring attention to their needs. This means you need to have a plan in place to keep the child quiet should a critical situation develop. It might be something simple like giving them a pacifier or it could be more complicated like giving a dose of antihistamine or other substance to cause them to become drowsy. Although talk to a doctor about this before giving any medications or making it a part of your emergency plan.

Non-battery Powered Toys - When a child's hands and minds are occupied the situation will become more bearable for both them and you. Plan on bringing at least one non-battery powered toy in the BOB to keep the child entertained while you set up camp. Ideally, you should choose a toy with many uses and ways to interact. A single, light toy is best; rather than something with many pieces. You should let your child pick the item and put it in the BOB themselves since they will understand that they are setting aside special toy for the family preparedness plan.

Comfort Item - Kids of this age are affected by the world around them and will know something is wrong. It is a good idea to pack a familiar item in the BOB so they can comfort themselves. This will make the situation less overwhelming for them and reduce your stress as well.

Child BOB - Most school-aged children carry their own backpack. Consider giving them their own BOB with a few supplies to help take the load off your own pack. You can help them pack their own clothes and other lightweight survival items. It is best to keep their load to about five pounds of gear as you don't want to give them too much.

BUG OUT PLANNING FOR SCHOOL AGED KIDS

This is the age when a child can start contributing to the family disaster preparation. They will often be able to do some tasks under adult supervision like collecting firewood, setting up camp, foraging, and other tasks. This is also a good age to start installing the survival mindset. Bring your child with you as you plan for your bug out and pack your gear.

Start teaching your child basic survival skills to get them involved. To start, train them with some basic first aid. This way they can provide you with some assistance if you get injured.

It is a good idea to put family photos in a child's pocket. In the event that you get separated from your kids, they will be able to show the photo to authorities to find you again.

While school-aged children can do more and have more initiative, remember you are still going to have to carry them at some point. You need to prepare your family BOB in a manner that won't prevent you from carrying your child when needed.

TWEEN AND TEENS AGE 10-18

By this age, a kid can carry their own personal gear rather than having it included in the family BOB. This can include spare clothes, rain gear, and any tools for their own use including hunting and self-defense. Get a backpack made for the smaller frame of your teen. In it, you can pack the following:

Hunting Tools - Teens are old enough to be taught minimum weapon safety, care, and use. However, this doesn't necessarily mean you need to give them a firearm. You can teach them to hunt with a slingshot or bow and arrow depending on your comfort level. Allow them to practice accuracy and stalking to regularly get them prepared for catching dinner while you're bugging out in an emergency.

Knife - This is a basic tool with limitless uses. You should teach a teen to safely carry, use, sharpen and care for a knife. Allow your teen to pack a knife if their BOB. There are numerous tasks a teen could do with a knife to assist the bug out group.

BUG OUT PLANNING FOR TWEENS AND TEENS

Teens are just starting adulthood, and this is a great time to start giving them responsibility. They will know the seriousness of a bug out situation and can understand that everyone needs to help each other. As you prepare for a disaster, challenge your teen to make decisions for themselves while in a controlled environment. This teaches them responsibility and caring for the family. You can also teach teens more advanced skills such as the following:

✧ Basic survival skills

✧ First aid

- ✧ Signaling

- ✧ Orienteering

- ✧ Fire building

- ✧ Scavenging

- ✧ Hunting

- ✧ Trapping

- ✧ Shelter building

This age group is also able to take on autonomous tasks when you're bugging out such as setting up a camp. They are also going to understand the dangers of a bug out situation so you can start teaching them self-defense.

Bugging out in an emergency with children of any age can present unique challenges to an already difficult and dangerous situation. However, with some planning, you can see how you can easily overcome these challenges and ensure your entire family is evacuated to safety.

Think carefully about what items you want to add to your family BOB to make things easier for everyone. When possible try to include your children in your disaster preparation steps and emergency planning, so everyone knows what to do when the time comes. Lastly, let's take a look at the BOB you need to pack for your pets.

When it comes to BOBs, most people don't often think that each of their pets needs a BOB as well. Let's take a look at how you can make your own pet BOB.

There are nearly 79 million dogs and 87 million cats in the United States alone. Nearly 39% of households have one dog, and 33% have one cat at least. If you have a pet, you know that they rely on you for their food, shelter, and safety. In the event of an emergency, you need to prepare and care for your pets just as you would for other human family members.

WHAT TO PACK FOR A DOG

- ✓ Owner contact information along with vaccine/medical records.

- ✓ Dog food and bowl as well as can opener and spoon if needed.

- ✓ Dog treats.

- ✓ Water with a bowl, enough water for 2.5 oz of water for every 1 oz of food.

- ✓ Protective clothing including raincoat and/or regular coat.

- ✓ Dog bed with an extra blanket.

- ✓ Carrier with handle.

- ✓ Collar with ID tag.

- ✓ Leash/harness.

- ✓ A tie-out.

- ✓ Muzzle.

- ✓ First aid kit.

- ✓ Daily medications.

- ✓ Clean up supplies.

- ✓ Grooming supplies if needed.

WHAT TO PACK FOR A CAT

- ✓ Owner contact information with vaccine/medical records.

- ✓ Cat food with the bowl as well as a can opener and spoon if needed.

- ✓ Cat treats.

- ✓ Water with a bowl, at least 2.5 oz of water for every 1 oz of food.

- ✓ Protective clothing such as a cat sweater if needed.

- ✓ Cat bed with a blanket.

- ✓ Carrier with handle.

- ✓ Collar with ID tag.

- ✓ First aid kit.

- ✓ Daily medications.

- ✓ Litter box/pan with cat litter.

- ✓ Clean up supplies.

- ✓ Grooming supplies if needed.

IDENTIFICATION AND DOCUMENTATION

Ideally, a pet should have an ID tag with some way for people to contact you. Cell phone numbers and addresses are a good idea. Carry a photo of your pets with you, so you can show people what to look for in case you lose your pet. You should also have vet records on hand. This will not only verify ownership but will also prove your pet is properly vaccinated.

You should also have your vet's phone number and any emergency number for after hours care. If you pet becomes ill or has any type of accident, call your vet first. They can give you additional instructions and let you know if you need to bring your pet to a vet. There are also poison control hotlines that you should have a phone number for at all times.

MEDICATIONS

As with humans, you should always have extra medication on hand in case you are unable to get a prescription refilled. In addition, you should consider having some activated charcoal on hand. You should always talk a vet before treating an animal for poison but having some activated charcoal on hand just in case you can't get a vet right away is important. The activated charcoal will help absorb the poison and can be a lifesaver for your pet. Your vet should be able to tell you the correct dosage based on your pet's size or you can ask about it during your next check up/follow up appointments.

FIRST AID KIT

While you will already be packing a first aid kit for humans; you still want to have a second one with pet specific items. Make sure you mark the first aid kit for pets differently so you can keep the supplies separate.

FOOD AND WATER

Having extra food is important in your emergency kit, for both humans and animals. You should never assume you'll just share your food with your pets. This will not only dwindle your supply sooner, but the combination of human food and stressful environment can cause your pets to have an upset stomach; leading to dehydration. Therefore, keep extra pet food on hand.

As with humans, clean drinking water is just as important as food. You can share the same water you drink with your pets. Calculate about how much your pet or pets will consume and add that amount to your supply. Just remember to bring a bowl.

CONFINEMENT

You should always bring some type of confinement or restraint for your pet. Most dogs can do fine with a well-fitting collar or harness and a leash. Cats and smaller dogs may need a crate or carrier. No matter which type you choose, make sure it is as escape proof as possible. The last thing you want to happen in a stressful survival situation is to have your dog slip out of their collar and run away from you. You may also want to pack an extra long leash in case you need to tie up your dog while camping out during your bug out after an emergency.

CREATE A PET EMERGENCY PLAN

Research has shown that about 50% or more pet owners don't have an emergency plan in place for their pets or have enough supplies on hand. As with human BOBs, a pet BOB needs to have the basic survival necessities for 72 hours. You should have an idea in place for long term survival as well, but generally the first two to three days are going to be the worst, and this is what the kit is for.

A medium-sized BOB for each pet will often be enough to fit everything they need with the exception of pet carriers. You can even buy a backpack for your own dog to carry their own supplies if they are big enough.

You can also choose to use a single bag with all the supplies for every pet in your home. It may seem like a lot of supplies, but it is well worth it for the health and safety of your furry family members. Now that we've covered all the necessary BOBs; let's take a look at the Every Day Carry (EDC) bag.

EVERYDAY CARRY (EDC) PACK

EVERYDAY Carry or EDC refers to a pack that carries gear on your person with you at all times. This typically includes gear that fits in pockets, backpacks, briefcases, etc. The overall goal of the EDC is to increase your quality of life, and every piece of gear should focus on this goal by increasing one of the following four:

1. Self-reliance

2. Security

3. Comfort

4. Safety

The choice of EDC gear is very personal and should be based on individual lifestyle, environment, and individual needs. The philosophy behind everyday carry gear is vastly different depending on the person. Some place emphasis on minimalism while others want gear that prepares them for every possible situation.

EDC ITEMS

Most EDC items should be both small in number and size; making them possible to carry on your person without needing to carry around another container. There are some that find it easier to carry all the items in a specific EDC bag and others who prefer to consolidate into as few multi-purpose tools as possible.

Before we look at the items in an EDC kit, you should consider the important aspects that make an item an EDC item. For something to be considered an EDC item it needs to meet one of the following criteria:

➢ They need to be small enough to carry with you in a pocket.

➢ They need to be useful for a SHTF scenario you may face.

➢ They need to act as a self-defense weapon.

➢ They need to help you open things, start a fire or fix things.

➢ They need to be able to cut things.

➢ They need to help you tie things.

➢ They need to help you filter water.

➢ They need to have a means of helping with communication.

PICKING EDC ITEMS TO CARRY

As we've already said, what you carry will depend on yourself, your location and your situation. A small

EDC can't prepare you for everything, but it can prepare you for the most important things that commonly happen around you. As you will see from the list of EDC items, they often have dozens of uses.

First, ask yourself what items you need to carry to accomplish your basic daily routine. These are the items that you can't leave your home without. At a minimum, this includes a wallet, keys, and phone. Depending on where you live, you might require more than this. These items need to be as minimal as possible since they are the core of your EDC kit.

Next, you need to ask yourself what are the threats, risks, and common problems that you are likely to face each day. Take a look at the environment around you and identify what negative events are most likely to happen. Once you have a list of medium to high-risk threats, add these to problems in your daily life. Are you frequently opening packages? Are you often in a dark area at night? This will help you determine the most important things to pack.

Then you need to ask yourself what you can carry that would help across many situations. Think of items that you can carry which have many uses. These would be items like duct tape, paracord, and a multi-tool.

Lastly, ask yourself what items you want to carry that will assist with low probability and high impact situations that you are likely to face. These are items that are nice to have, but you hope you won't have to use them unless you are under extreme circumstances. These would be items such as a seatbelt cutter/window breaker etc.

When you carefully consider the above areas, you will be able to put together a list of EDC items. Remember you aren't trying to solve all problems or cover every possible incidence with an EDC kit, for that, you have your BOB at home. The EDC is supposed to be as simple and effective as possible. It is designed to carry the items every day so you don't want an extensive list of items you may never use.

ASSESSING RISK

Rating the risk of threats in your area is a good way to judge if an item needs to be included in your EDC or even your BOB contents. You can judge each threat by using two criteria.

PROBABILITY

Ask yourself what are the chances of a threat occurring? Is it highly probable and something you see happening once a week or several times a month? Is it something you'll only see once a year or every several years? Rate the probability of threats based on their realistic occurrence and your experience as well as what has historically happened in your area.

If a threat actually happens, what would be the impact of it? How easy would it be to overcome? Does it have the potential to be fatal? The following link will take you to a good Threat Assessment Matrix that can help you determine the level of threats:

http://www.thebugoutbagguide.com/wp-content/uploads/2013/12/Threat-Assessment-V2.pdf

GEAR TO HELP WITH THESE THREATS

Once you have determined what threats you are most likely to face, then you need to determine what gear you can carry that will help with these threats. These EDC items should assist in the threats you are most likely to face and help make your life easier.

Folding Knife - Having a folding knife is key in an EDC kit since it serves a variety of purposes and can help with a number of tasks.

Flashlight - You never know when you'll be caught in a blackout or if you'll have to walk to your car at night after a long day at work. Having a good LED flashlight in your EDC kit will not only help light your way through but will also make a good self-defense tool.

Multi-Tool - This jack-of-all-trades tool has a low profile and great functionality to help with a variety of tasks.

Next would be items that help with rare and high consequence problems. Tools in this category would consist of the following:

Tactical Pen - This is a high-grade metal pen that can be used as a self-defense tool and glass breaking aid when needed.

Pry Tool - This helps you to open doors or containers should you come across a car accident or problem in your home.

Paracord - This wonderful product is light yet strong and won't rot. It has nearly as many uses as duct tape. Having a little of this on hand will allow you to make a splint or shelter in an emergency.

HOW BIG SHOULD YOUR EDC KIT BE?

Once you have determined your list of EDC gear, determining the best EDC bag size to fit everything should be relatively simple. It is best to find the smallest bag possible to fit all of your gear. Start by measuring the largest item to get the minimum dimensions for your EDC bag.

Also keep in mind if you are going to be adding items on an occasional basis to your kits such as rain gear, water bottles, food, documents or anything else as the need arises.

If you want extra space or the option of modular additions, then consider a MOLLE system. EDC bags come in a variety of styles and sizes; from a small organizer pouch that you can put in a cargo pocket on your pants up to a 30-liter backpack. Anything larger than this and you're looking at a GHB or BOB. If you have items that won't fit into these, then you need to re-evaluate the items on your EDC gear list.

CHOOSING THE BEST EDC BAG

As we've said, there are many bags that can be used for EDC purposes. Let's look at the most common EDC bag types.

EDC ORGANIZER POUCH

This is the smallest type of EDC bag. This is ideal for those who have too many items to just carry them in their pockets, but not enough to require a full pack. These bags are typically identified by the following:

➢ One liter or less in volume.

➢ Many interior pockets, hooks, and webbing for organizing gear.

➢ A MOLLE attachment for integration into larger kits.

➢ Can fit in a cargo pocket or is worn on a belt.

Common items carried in this bag include the following:

- ✓ Folding knife

- ✓ Compass

- ✓ Tactical pen

- ✓ Waterproof notebook

- ✓ First aid items

- ✓ Glasses

- ✓ Phone

- ✓ Keys

- ✓ Multi-tool

- ✓ Lighter

- ✓ Credit cards

- ✓ Cash

- ✓ Survival whistle

EDC LUMBAR PACK

These are larger than the organizer pouch but are smaller than a sling bag or backpack. These are a good option if you plan on carrying larger items or a greater amount of smaller items. Since this type of bags do not strap around the arms or shoulders and are ideal for those who need a full range of motion. These bags are typically identified by the following:

- ➤ 5-10 liters in volume.

- ➢ Worn around the waist and has a carry handle if you need to carry by hand.

- ➢ MOLLE webbing to attach them to larger bags or to attach smaller pouches.

- ➢ Multiple compartments each with various webbings, pouches, hooks, etc.

Common items carried in this pack include the following:

- ✓ Fixed blade knife

- ✓ First aid kit

- ✓ Handgun

- ✓ EDC flashlight

- ✓ Tablet

- ✓ E-reader

- ✓ Lock pick set

- ✓ Camera

- ✓ Full sized notepad

- ✓ Rain gear

- ✓ Rations

- ✓ Water bottle

✓ Gloves

EDC SLING BAG

This bag is typically used for heavier items due to its shoulder design. These are designed to be comfortable when carried a long distance with a heavy load. This makes them the best EDC bag for those who need to carry many items on a daily basis.

These bags are typically identified by the following:

➤ 10-20 liters in volume.

➤ MOLLE integration capacity.

➤ Allow left, or right side carry.

➤ Easy to secure tightly to the body.

➤ Many pockets and compartments for easy organization of gear.

Common items carried in this bag include the following:

✓ Extra ammunition

✓ Small laptop

✓ Mid-sized medical kit

✓ Prepackaged meals

✓ Paracord

- ✓ Fire starters
- ✓ Pry tool

EDC BACKPACK

This is the best option for those who want to pack a lot of gear just in case. It is the obvious choice if someone has large sized everyday carry items or a long list of EDC items based on their individual needs.

These bags are typically identified by the following:

- ➤ 20-30 liters in volume.
- ➤ MOLLE integration capability.
- ➤ Includes a hydration bladder system.
- ➤ Fewer pockets, but more modular customization possibilities for external pouches.

Common items carried in this bag include the following:

- ✓ Everything from the above three lists.
- ✓ Folding saw or hatchet
- ✓ Hydration bladder
- ✓ Change of clothes
- ✓ Full sized laptop

✓ Full medical kit

✓ Mini survival kit

EDC BAG FEATURES

This is where personal choice really takes effect. It is best to carry the smallest bag that meets your everyday needs. Thankfully, many good EDC bags have customization options that allow you to add or remove space as needed by modular MOLLE pouches so you can change based on your changing requirements.

No matter what bag style you choose from the list above there are features both good and bad when choosing a specific EDC bag for your personal needs.

ESSENTIAL FEATURES

Good Craftsmanship - If you plan on carrying your items every day then you don't want a cheap EDC bag that will fall apart at some point. Rather you want to invest in a quality bag from a brand that has a good reputation behind it, and it will pay off in the long run.

MOLLE Integration - This is a valuable feature to have in any disaster preparedness bag since it allows for limitless customization options. When you have it as a part of your EDC kit, it allows flexible adaptation no matter what bag size and style you choose. This allows you to change as your EDC needs change.

Hydration System - This option is only available for sling bags and backpacks. However, if you have one of these built into your bag, and then you will save space and reduce the need to carry a water bottle. You should consider this feature if you potentially need to cover large distances with your EDC kit.

Adjustable Fit - Everyone has a different body shape and structure. If you buy a bag that is meant to fit everyone, you are only going to have frustration and discomfort. For an EDC bag to be good, it needs to fit your unique body shape without restricting your movement. This means at a minimum it should have three multiple adjustment straps at the shoulders, hips, and sternum.

Organization - A good indication of a high-quality EDC bag rather than a general consumer bag is that it is well laid out, accessible, and practical when it comes to the organizational features built into the bag. This allows you to find the EDC items you need when you need them and allows you to organize them in a logical way. Most quality EDC bags will have a variety of webbing, pouches, Velcro, zippers, sleeves and compartments to store various EDC gear.

Quality Zippers - The zipper is always the weakest point of any bag. Since you are going to use them thousands of times during the life of the bag, you want to choose an EDC bag that has strong zippers. It is best to have zippers with pulls made from strong plastic, aluminum or other rust-free material.

If you carry these bags every day, they will be exposed to the elements. Over time corrosion and failure can happen in cheap zippers.

UNNECESSARY FEATURES

As important as it is to have essential features, it is also important to identify unnecessary features. These can end up costing you more for an EDC bag than you have to pay. Be aware of and avoid the following features when choosing an EDC bag.

Single Compartment - If you are going to carry EDC gear in a bag that only has one single, large compartment then everything is going to get mixed together. Then when you need things during an emergency you won't be able to get to it quickly. In addition, these bags can sometimes be uncomfortable to carry. A bag with multiple compartments and organizational options is the better choice for an EDC bag.

Elastic Straps - This is one of the areas where a manufacturer will cut costs. Rather than making a bag with strong, padded and adjustable straps; a cheap bag uses elastic straps that make the bag a so-called one-size-fits-all. Also, the elasticity wears out over time causing the bag to hand lower than desired. Avoid a bag with elastic straps at all costs.

Large Bags - An EDC kit is never intended to cover all possible circumstances. That is why you have a BOB. Therefore, you should assess your needs and minimize what gear you are carrying. You should never need to carry anything bigger than a backpack.

As you can tell, a lot goes into finding the best EDC bag to meet your needs. It is made both easier and more difficult because the majority of the decisions are a highly personal choice. You will have to balance your needs versus your personal preferences to determine the best EDC bag for your needs. Now let's take a look at the GHB.

GET HOME BAG (GHB)

WHEN WAS the last time you had a flat tire or ran out of gas? These were likely a minor issue that you were able to resolve easily. However, there are plenty of other emergencies that can happen today which aren't as easy to resolve. In an SHTF scenario or during a natural disaster, the 911 communications system is filled with callers and cell phones can eventually go dead.

No matter what emergency hits your area, you are going to need to be prepared to survive. Most people falsely assume that they'll be home when something really bad happens. But the reality is, it is highly likely that you won't be home when a major emergency happens. Do you know what to do if an emergency happens while you're at work or driving home after work? Even if you only work an hour away from home, this can turn into a major trek if a natural disaster occurs.

WHAT IS A GET HOME BAG?

A Get Home Bag (GHB) is similar to the EDC bag but takes survival a step further. Most of the us spend a good portion of our time at work. The job can be anywhere, but it is often some distance from home. Often there is different terrain and/or an urban environment between your work and home. The GHB is what you'll use if a disaster happens and you need to get home.

A GHB should have the supplies you need to get home from wherever you are and should have the basic tools needed to help you escape in the event of a disaster. The GHB should stay at your place of work or maybe even in your car. The bag should be similar to a BOB, but easy to store in your office and as normal looking as possible.

BUILDING A GHB GEAR LIST

The contents of a GHB will vary greatly depending on where you live and the type of emergencies and/or disasters you want to prepare for. You'll also need to consider your daily commute and improvised ways to get home if other kinds of transit become unavailable.

Consider the following when developing a get home plan.

1. What terrain are you going to travel through wilderness, suburbs, and urban cities?

2. Are there any major waterways: do you need to cross or devise routes around?

3. How many hours would it take you to walk home?

There are some basic tools and supplies that should be packed in a standard GHB. Additional item and exact contents may change depending on the distance from your work to home and the type of terrain you may be covering.

Water - You need at least one liter of water ideally kept in a metal container in case you need to cook or boil water in it. You should also carry a personal water filter. Best of all you should have the skill to find alternative sources of water.

Food - Most of the time you are only going to be on the road for several hours. For a GHB the recommendation is to pack at least three days worth of food. If you can't get home in that amount of time you can stretch it to last twice as long. The main concern about having food in your GHB is to maintain your energy levels. For this reason, the food needs to be energy-packed snacks such as nuts, trail mix, or beef jerky.

Shelter - The GHB is designed to get you home quickly enough, so you will likely get home to your BOB before needing any shelter. However, if you do get stuck for an extended period of time then you at least want some plastic sheeting or a tarp along with some paracord or clothesline to build a shelter when needed.

Fire - The ability to build a fire is important for both warmth and cooking; making it one of the most important survival skills. You should pack at least two methods for fire starting as well as some form of tinder in case you don't have any readily available.

Clothing - Often the clothes you wear to work aren't going to be suitable for a sudden change in weather or well suited to a survival situation. Therefore, you'll want to change clothes as soon as it is safe to do so. You don't need to change clothes every day in a survival situation, so one or two changes of clothes are all you need.

First Aid Kit - A basic small first aid kit is all you need. You should also have a good knowledge of first aid treatment. Along with this, you should have an emergency blanket and a dust mask.

Self Defense - In the wilderness, there can be dangerous animals, and in the urban setting, there can be dangerous humans. For this reasons, you want to pack a self-defense item. A weapon should always be your last line of defense, but it is best to have one if needed. Remember to check local laws. Since you'll be leaving your GHB at work, you want to make sure the weapon is properly secured.

Communications - In a disaster, a lot of communication methods such as landline phones, cell phones, and Internet connections can be lost. News broadcasts on AM/FM radio will keep you up to date on what's going on around you. Pack an emergency radio that has a hand crank and a rechargeable battery.

Headlamp - In survival situations a good flashlight or headlamp is important. A headlamp can be the best option since it leaves your hands free to work on getting out of the building.

CHOOSING A BAG FOR YOUR GHB

When it comes to your GHB, there are several types of packs you can choose from. Each pack will have its own pros and cons. In the end, the bag you choose should be best suited to you and your unique situation. Consider the following bags when choosing your GHB.

Backpack - This is a great option for hands-free carrying and providing extra space for additional gear. It also allows you to run and climb easily. However, it isn't that easy to access contents and isn't as discreet.

Messenger Bag - This option provides great access while on the move, has plenty of pockets for organization and doesn't look like a survival kit. However, it is difficult to run with and can be uncomfortable over long distances since the weight isn't evenly distributed.

Lumbar Pack - The option is compact and easily accessible with external straps that can carry extra clothing. However, it places all the weight on your hips with no room for additional items.

PACKING YOUR GHB

Packing your GHB is perhaps just as important as determining what you put into it. It is important to keep in mind that your GHB shouldn't be as big or as full of supplies as your BOB. Even with fewer supplies, knowing how to pack it all into a GHB can be a bit overwhelming. The basic way to pack a GHB is to have heavier and less frequently used items on the bottom with the lighter and more frequent items towards the top.

If you are overwhelmed, you can start by sorting your GHB items into three piles. The first pile will be your basic essentials that you will need if it takes you over a day to get home. This is everything you won't need to access right away. The second pile will be for regular use items. These items you will need if it takes you more than three hours to get home. Lastly, you have a pile of urgent items or things you will need to access right away when a disaster happens. These are items you will likely need no matter how long it takes you to get home.

HELPFUL TIPS

The most important thing is to make sure your bag isn't too heavy. A GHB shouldn't weigh over twenty pounds. If your bag is too heavy, reconsider what you have packed in it.

Make sure you protect everything in your pack from moisture. Use Ziploc bags to seal important items and protect them in the event of rain or other moisture.

Disasters can occur at any time and place. During an unexpected event, you need to remain calm and use the gear in your GHB to get home as quickly and safely as possible. Now we will consider the biggest bag of them all, the INCH bag.

I'M NEVER COMING HOME (INCH) BAG

SO WE'VE covered the BOB, EDC, and GHB; do we really need another bag? Each bag has their own purpose and usefulness, but you don't necessarily need all of them. Your individual needs and location will determine which types of bags are best for you. But before you make your decision we have one more to consider.

The INCH bag or I'm Never Coming Home is the bag to pack if you aren't going to pack any other. Or if you already have a BOB, then most of your work is already done. The INCH bag is different from a BOB because it is bigger, has more items and is designed to keep you safe and alive no matter where you bug out to.

CHOOSING AN INCH BAG

There is no shortage of backpacks to choose from, but there are a few questions you want to consider to make sure you are choosing the right bag for your needs.

➢ Does the bag fit properly and distribute the weight appropriately?

➢ Does it have adequate supports?

> ➤ Are there enough compartments and pockets to store everything?

> ➤ Is it durable and waterproof?

> ➤ Is it able to contain everything you need to survive?

While you need a bag with plenty of room, you also don't want to buy one that is too big. Keep in mind you are going to have to carry this bag, fully loaded, for extended periods. The total weight of an INCH bag shouldn't exceed 25% of your total body weight.

THE CONTENTS OF AN INCH BAG

When it comes to the contents of an INCH bag, your priority is on basic survival gear over luxury or comfort items. For this, you will need the following:

- ✓ Gas mask

- ✓ Disposable surgical masks

- ✓ Emergency blankets

- ✓ Small tent

- ✓ Sleeping bag

- ✓ Waterproof groundsheet

- ✓ Tarp

- ✓ Two methods of starting a fire

- ✓ Water
- ✓ Water purification method
- ✓ Food
- ✓ Tactical stove
- ✓ Utensils for cooking and eating
- ✓ A kettle
- ✓ Mugs and plates
- ✓ Fishing kit
- ✓ Hunting knives
- ✓ Whetstone
- ✓ Guns and ammo
- ✓ Traps or snares
- ✓ Edible plant guide for your area
- ✓ First aid kit
- ✓ Toilet paper
- ✓ Brush, comb, and mirror
- ✓ Toothbrush, toothpaste, and dental floss
- ✓ Bar of soap
- ✓ Wet wipes
- ✓ Shampoo

- ✓ Deodorant
- ✓ Hand sanitizer
- ✓ Disposable razors
- ✓ Pocket-sized tissue packs
- ✓ Nail cutters
- ✓ Towel
- ✓ Clothing
- ✓ Extra shoelaces
- ✓ Sunglasses
- ✓ Hiking boots
- ✓ Wet weather gear
- ✓ Work gloves
- ✓ Hatchet
- ✓ Garbage bags
- ✓ Pencils
- ✓ Multi-purpose tool
- ✓ Hardware items
- ✓ Measuring tape
- ✓ Sewing kit
- ✓ Duct tape

- ✓ Small folding saw
- ✓ Crow bar/hammer
- ✓ Screwdriver set
- ✓ Wire cutters
- ✓ Ziploc bags
- ✓ Assortment of batteries
- ✓ Hand crank and/or solar powered flashlight
- ✓ Rope/paracord
- ✓ Orienteering compass
- ✓ Topographic maps
- ✓ GPS system
- ✓ Distress flares
- ✓ Survival whistle
- ✓ Cell phone and extra battery
- ✓ Solar powered charger for phone
- ✓ Headlamp
- ✓ Small emergency radio, hand crank or solar powered
- ✓ Cash
- ✓ Passport/ID/vital information and documents

As you can tell from this list, the INCH bag is truly all inclusive and is only missing the kitchen sink. However, the main limitations to the INCH bag are going to be space, weight and the money you want to put into it. This list could actually be much longer, but the focus is only to pack what you need to survive or get you by until you can learn to survive with what is around you. Now that you know all the different bags there is just one more to consider, the vehicle BOB. Again just to remind you, I am no way suggesting that you should prepare each and every bag I am mentioning here, but I am merely suggesting you consider each and decide which ones are appropriate for your needs.

VEHICLE BOB

W HILE CALLED a vehicle BOB, this isn't really a BOB which is why it wasn't put in that category. Rather this is a kit that is placed in your car in the event of an emergency situation.

VEHICLE BOB ITEMS

There are a lot of supplies that can be kept in your car as a part of a vehicle BOB. However, keep in mind the amount of space you have in your car. The following are some items to consider when putting together your vehicle BOB. These are just the basics, but you might have others that meet your specific needs.

- Storage - Box, bag or container to keep your supplies.

- Physical Needs - Food and water.

- Medical Supplies - First aid kit, prescription medications, hygiene products.

- Extra Clothing - Coats, blankets, socks, gloves, shoes, etc.

- Automobile Care - Jumper cables, fix-a-flat, functional spare tire, tool set, fire extinguisher, oil/other fluids.

- ➤ Signals - Whistle, road flares, pen/marker, paper/cardboard, cell phone battery and charger, emergency radio, flashlights or spotlight, headlamp.

- ➤ Survival Tools - Ax or knife, rope/paracord, matches or lighter, heat source, flashlights and extra batteries.

PREVENTION IS KEY

Prevention is the key to avoiding unnecessary problems. Be sure to perform regular maintenance on your vehicle. Change your oil, check tire pressure and make sure your car can handle the daily use and weather conditions you face. Disaster preparedness is a matter of life and death. When you have a good plan in place and properly packed bags, you'll be better prepared than most. Now let's start looking at the individual gear selection.

BLADED TOOLS

FIXED BLADE KNIFE

THERE IS a lot of gear that goes into all the bags we've discussed, but the most versatile and reliable item you can pack is a knife. Finding the best fixed blade knife is often at the top of the list when choosing gear for a survival kit. There are many survival applications for a fixed blade knife and it doesn't take up too much room in any pack. Let's take a look at how you can choose a great fixed blade knife for your packs.

PRACTICAL USES

This fixed blade knife is often associated with the survival practice of bushcraft. If you read my Bushcraft book, then you know I spoke at length about the importance of this knife and the use of it. There are some who travel into the wilderness with only a knife as their only survival tool. There are also a great number of urban tasks you can do with a knife.

Let's take a look at a few of these tasks:

- Prying doors and windows

- Breaking glass

- Cleaning game

- Hunting

- Makeshift spear

- Shelter building

- Self defense

- Cutting rope

- Chopping small wood

- Batoning through branches

- Opening containers and cans

- Preparing food

- Eating

- Hammering

FIXED BLADE VS. FOLDING KNIVES

If you're like me, you're wondering why a fixed blade knife and not a folding knife. Folding knives are more compact and lightweight; two factors we've already discussed are very important. However, a fixed blade knife does have more advantages in a survival situation.

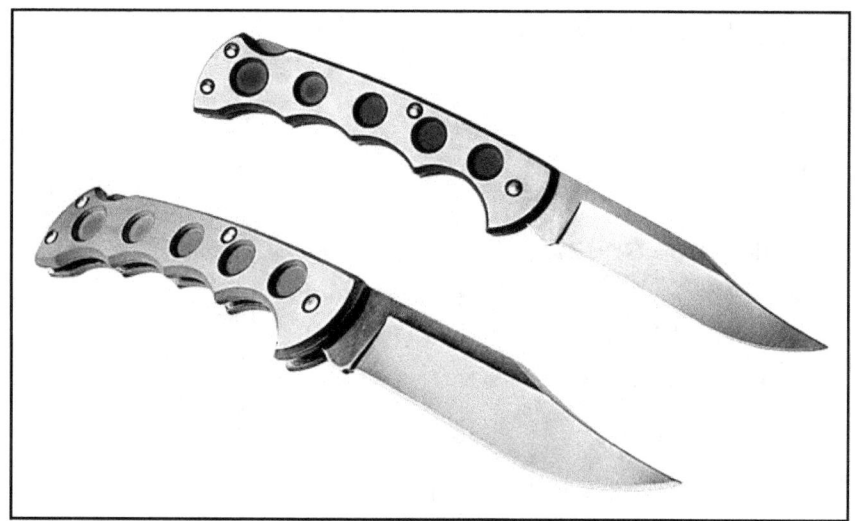

Strength - If you are going to be putting your survival knife through hard use such as the applications listed above, then you want a strong knife. A folding knife has a hinge that pivots around and is a major point of weakness in the design. A folding knife works well enough for fine, detailed work or general everyday use; but if you want to use your knife for heavier work, then you want a fixed blade knife.

Size - Even a small fixed blade knife is going to be longer and heavier than the biggest folding knife. Again this is an advantage when doing hard work. Longer knife length gives you greater leverage if you need to pry things and better advantage in self-defense or hunting. The small additional weight of a fixed blade knife doesn't significantly impact the ability to carry your bag, but it will come in handy in a survival situation.

Maintenance - This is another advantage a fixed blade knife has over a folding knife. The hinge and locking mechanism in a folding knife can clog with dirt and sand or corrode. This can make it difficult or impossible to use a folding knife. A fixed blade knife won't fail on you. Simplicity is better.

HANDLE OPTIONS

When it comes to choosing a fixed blade knife you have two handle categories to consider: tang and grip. Let's look at each individually to determine which is best for your particular situation.

KNIFE TANG

The tang is the part of the knife that extends from the base of the blade guard to the butt of the knife. The tang is typically covered by the knife's handle or wrapped in paracord. All knives have three varieties of Tang: full, partial and hollow.

Full - This knife has a solid piece of metal that extends from the hand guard all the way to the butt of the knife. These knives are often a single piece of steel that makes up both the blade and tang. This is the strongest option of the knife and is best for those who want a heavy duty knife that is used for major tasks.

Partial - This is when the blade steel extends only part of the way into the handle. Some manufacturers use this as a way to cut costs and are often the sign of a cheap knife. These knives are okay for light duty work, but shouldn't be used for survival purposes.

Hollow - There is still much debate over a hollow handled survival knife. These are going to be weaker than a full tang knife. To make this judgment, you need to consider what you plan to use the knife for. You can likely get away with light duties, but you probably shouldn't use it for anything heavier such as hammering or prying. With a hollow handle knife, you do have the option of storing something in the cavity such as the following:

➢ Map

➢ Fishing kit

➢ Fire starter

➢ First aid items

➢ Paracord

GRIP OPTIONS

There are also many materials that can be used to make a knife grip. The most practical and cost-effective options are Micarta, Glass Reinforced Nylon, G-10, and Zytel. Sometimes it simply comes down to how the grip feels in your hand. You want a knife that gives you a good feel and can be easily handled with and without gloves. You also want a knife with a good guard. When you get all of these elements together, you will be able to find the best fixed blade knife for your kit. Take the time to carefully consider your choices.

SIZE AND WEIGHT

There is no perfect length or weight for a fixed blade knife. The ideal size will depend on what you are going to use it for. Let's look at how knife size will impact your decision.

LENGTH

A longer fixed blade knife, one over ten inches in overall length, is often heavier and takes up more space in your kit. However, longer knives can be better at heavy work and self-defense. By comparison, a shorter knife is good for finer detail and takes up less room. Again it all comes down to how you plan to use your knife. Weigh the pros and cons when determining which knife is best for you.

WEIGHT

When assessing knife weight, you need to find the right balance. No one wants to carry more gear than they need to and this includes choosing a knife that is heavier. As with everything else, finding the best weight comes down to how you are going to use the knife.

A lighter knife will cause less fatigue while carrying and using it. Lighter is also better for detail work. Heavier knives give you a greater force for heavy work. For light work, you want a knife that is less than 12 oz and heavier for a knife that will be used for more brute force.

BLADE OPTIONS

When you include fixed blade tactical, bushcraft and hunting knives, there are countless blade options. This wide selection can be a great way to customize your knife to meet your specific needs. Let's take a look at blade options.

Drop Point - This is a great all around option if you want a multipurpose knife. They typically have a gradual curve along their spine and a wide belly. This means they are easy to control and highly versatile.

Serrated - Full or partial serration on a knife allows for faster cutting of human-made materials. These blades also tend to stay sharp longer.

Gut Hook - This is a special type of blade where the back of the blade or the spine, has a sharpened indentation or hook. This is often used when opening the abdomen of an animal during field dressing. This is a popular option for those who need a hunting knife.

Tanto - This is a flat edge rather than a curved edge, and it comes to a triangular point. This gives the blade better strength when piercing materials. This makes them good for those who want a tactical knife.

Chisel Tip - This is a flat tip that has been sharpened to allow the user to make digging cuts. This option is also very strong at times when the knife is used as a prying tool. It is a popular search and rescue option or urban knife.

Clip Point - This knife has a curved or straight section running from mid-spine to the tip of the blade. This allows for optimal control in the point while cutting as well as good piercing. This is another popular option for those wanting a bushcraft knife or a hunting knife.

SHEATH OPTIONS

We have talked a lot about finding the perfect fixed blade knife. However, another important aspect is how you are going to carry the knife. Many people focus on finding the right knife and just take the sheath that comes with it. Most quality knives do come with a reliable sheath, but it is worth it to consider some other options if you want the best in a sheath.

Attachment - How are you planning to carry your knife or keep it in your kit? It is important to choose a sheath that can accommodate the way you plan to carry it. Good knives typically have a knife with more than one carry option. If you need to get a sheath look for one with multiple carry options or MOLLE integration to keep your carry options open.

Material - There are a few materials that can be used to make a sheath. Kydex is a type of plastic that is molded to fit the shape of the knife. This option is lightweight and nearly indestructible. Another type is nylon. This woven material is lightweight, inexpensive and very durable.

Most of these types come with MOLLE integration and attach to a belt or bag through Velcro or snap-secured straps. Lastly, there is leather. This is a classic sheath material. It is tough, but not as lightweight as nylon. You should get a leather sheath with straps and buckles to attach it.

LEGALITY

Before you purchase a fixed blade knife make sure you check your local ownership and carry laws to ensure that it is legal. You can also contact your local police department for more information.

As you can see, there is a lot that goes into choosing the best fixed blade knife for your survival kit. Just remember to focus on the basics and take into account specifically what you want to use it for. This will allow you to choose the best fixed blade knife for your needs. If you are going to also need a pocket knife, there are a few other things to consider.

Pocket knives have many uses in a survival situation. These knives combine the utility of a knife with compact size and weight. Some people choose to carry a pocket knife as a backup to a larger blade while others use the pocket knife as their main knife. Either way, having a pocket knife can be a great addition to any survival kit. Let's look at a few options and see which ones are good for your needs.

COMPACT AND LIGHTWEIGHT

If you are going to carry your pocket knife often as an alternative to having to carry a larger knife, then you want to maximize the benefits of a pocket knife. First, you don't want to carry around a pocket knife that is as heavy as a fixed blade knife. This means you want to find a pocket knife made of lighter materials like strong plastic or ones with a skeleton design to save weight. You also want to choose a knife that is five inches or less when folded so it can easily fit in a pocket or on a belt.

SINGLE HANDED OPENING

This is important when dealing with folding knives. If you need a survival knife in a hurry, you don't want a complicated knife that is difficult to open. You should be able to open the folding knife with either hand. The actual method for opening a knife with one hand will depend on your comfort and dexterity.

LOCKING MECHANISM

Just as important as the method for opening a knife, you also want a good locking mechanism. A cheap folding knife is going to fail and close on your hand at the worst possible time. When selecting a survival tool that you can rely on, you need to find a good locking mechanism. There are many ways the knife industry has worked to offer this and a good survival pocket knife has a multiple, redundant locking mechanism that basically engages to turn your folding knife into a fixed blade knife.

CONSTRUCTION

As with all survival gear here, spending a little extra for quality will improve your odds of getting great gear. Name brand knives from manufacturers with a great reputation are going to hold their edge longer and be less likely to have hinge problems compare than cheaper knives. Some of the signs to look for when identifying quality knives include the following:

✧ Screws or bolts for binding and not gluing.

✧ Fluid closing and opening of the blade.

✧ Holds an edge well with easy sharpening.

✧ A reliable locking mechanism.

✧ A comfortable and ergonomic grip that discourages your hand from slipping.

✧ Good quality steel or composite metal.

ADDITIONAL FEATURES FOR URBAN SURVIVAL

When it comes to choosing a folding knife, there are additional features that you may want to consider for specific situations. One of these would be individuals using the knife for urban survival. Some additional features that would be helpful would be the following.

Seatbelt / Line Cutter - This helps you to get out of a vehicle faster if you run into a survival scenario while in your car. This is often done with a narrow cutout on the back of the knife that can be used while the blade is folded to slide materials into it to cut.

Glass Breaker - Again this can help with evacuating from a vehicle or building during an urban survival situation.

Pry Tip - This is often a flat tip on a thicker blade that allows you to open doors and containers. However, you will often be trading the knife's ability to stab and poke. Although it can still be a good secondary knife for your survival kit.

ADDITIONAL FEATURES FOR WILDERNESS SURVIVAL

Partial Serration - This gives you the advantages of both a straight edge and serrated knives. Serration allows for the faster-cutting ability of things that you may face in a wilderness survival scenario.

Gut Hook - This helps you address wild game quicker. A lot of hunting and fishing knives have this option, but if your survival pocket knife is going to be your go-to blade, then this feature can be important for a survival knife.

There are plenty of survival pocket knives on the market, and it can be difficult to choose just one for your survival situation. Make sure you consider all of the essential features we discussed when choosing the ideal knife based on your survival scenario. Now that we've looked at the two main types of knives let's see which is best for the most important kit, the EDC.

EDC KNIFE

An EDC kit isn't complete without a knife, and there is a good chance you'll be using it on a daily basis for a variety of tasks so you should take the time to choose a great option. While we've already discussed fixed blade and folding knives, let's take a moment to consider both in the context of an EDC knife and how you can choose the best one for your needs. When you choose the right EDC knife, you will be able to make everyday tasks easier and give you an advantage in survival situations.

FIXED OR FOLDING

Perhaps the most important first choice you will make with an EDC knife is whether you want one that is fixed blade or folding. Most people choose a folding knife since it is smaller and easier to fit in a pocket or clip onto a belt. As with most features, it comes down to personal preference and the environment you typically live and work in when choosing which option is best for you.

For those in an urban environment, a folding EDC knife might be the better option since it is unobtrusive and lighter to carry. Being discreet is a must in urban areas. On the other hand, a fixed blade knife is easier in a rural setting and is less taboo in culture.

SIZE AND WEIGHT

The best EDC knife is going to be one that fits in a pocket or EDC kit and has strong, lightweight materials. It is important to keep in mind the everyday aspect of a knife when choosing it for an EDC kit. No one wants added weight in their pocket every day. A good EDC knife is one that is under five ounces and less than five inches to make carrying comfortable and easy.

EDGE

As we've already discussed, there are three types of blades available: full ground edge, full serration, and partial serration. Full ground edge is good for pushing cuts, scraping, precision work, poking, skewering and stabbing. Full serration is good for slicing through materials, but it poor for stabbing. Partial serration is a choice for most since it offers the advantages of both the previous edge types.

OPENING AND LOCKING METHODS

As we discussed when talking about folding knives, the opening and locking methods are very important. A blade should be easy to open and stay open until you decide to close it. Let's look at the following locking mechanisms.

Slip Joint Lock - This option is more than a century old. This is most typical of all the old-fashioned pocket knives. It is a simple design that is time tested. It is spring-loaded and requires a minimum of effort to open and close.

Ball Detent Mechanism - This option works similar to how a socket is locked on a socket wrench.

Liner Lock - This option requires adequate force to bypass the mechanism but is easier to close than a slip joint lock.

Frame Lock - This is called the integral lock. It uses a ball detent apparatus built into the handle, and it is spring loaded like a liner lock.

Axis Lock - This option uses a modified roller detent mechanism similar to those you see on car doors.

When it comes to opening mechanisms, there are three basic categories: manual, assisted and automatic. The best way to determine which of these three is best for you is to simply go to the store and try the various methods to see which you are most comfortable with.

GRIP STYLE AND MATERIAL

When it comes to choosing the grip for your EDC knife, there are two categories to consider: grip and material. You want a grip that fits well in your hand and allows for a secure grip under extreme and adverse conditions. The materials are what the grip is made from, and there are a variety of choices. We briefly touched on materials earlier, but we'll provide a bit more of a breakdown here:

G10 - Epoxy and fiberglass resin that is strong and lightweight.

Micarta - A mix of cloth linen or canvas and resin. Also a strong and lightweight option.

Titanium - This is an extremely strong and lightweight option that is virtually impervious to rust.

Carbon Fiber - This is a lightweight material, but it can also be very brittle. It is often more expensive and showy when compared to other materials.

Zytel - This is a lightweight and nearly indestructible plastic.

COST

Knives are certainly one of the gear items where you get what you pay for. While you may be able to find a decent EDC knife for under $50, the best are going to cost you more. When you are going to be carrying something every day, you will be better off paying a little more to get a high-quality EDC knife that will last you for years to come. A great knife is going to need less maintenance and can last for generations if taken proper care of. View your EDC knife as a lifelong investment.

A knife is certainly a valuable tool in your survival kit. However, if you are going to be in a rural area, you may want to consider additional bladed tools. Let's consider the ax next.

In a rural setting where firewood is your only true source of heat and cooking, an ax is a very useful tool that can potentially mean the difference between life and death. This is why you want to carefully choose the right ax for your survival kit. There are just a few points to consider.

BASICS

Most people have seen or held an ax at least once before, so I assume you too should know what we are talking about in this section. If you don't, you should know the major parts of an ax and how they affect it.

HANDLE

Many axes today still have a solid wooden handle that is often made from straight-grain hickory. These are sturdy and durable when treated correctly. There are a few alternative materials such as metal and fiberglass. The difference is often in how force is delivered and how you feel the recoil after repeated blows. It is best to choose an ax with the proper curve for what you are doing; we'll get more into that when we discuss uses.

HEAD

You want an ax that has a forged steel head and is securely fastened to the handle. You'll even find some axes that are a single piece of metal from the head to the handle. The size of the ax head will vary depending on what purpose you use it for. You don't want too large of a head if you're not going to need it since this will just increase your discomfort and fatigue, but a head that is too small can break easily.

TYPES OF AXES

HATCHET

This is a small, lightweight ax that is ideal for BOB and can also be carried on a belt. Often these are used for limbing trees, cutting kindling and for defense if necessary. The head of a hatchet is often one to one and a half pounds with a ten to fourteen-inch handle. While good for small jobs, don't expect to cut down a tree with this option.

FELLING AX

This option is typically used to cut down or fell trees. This ax is designed to cut across a grain of wood and can have one or two cutting heads. They come in a variety of weights, shapes, and handles. For a felling ax to work, it needs to be very sharp. The head is often three to four pounds, and the length is about thirty inches. This is the typical ax that most people think of.

FOREST AX

This is a cross between a felling ax and a hatchet. It can be used for everything from cutting kindling to cutting down smaller trees. While a little larger than a hatchet, it can still be carried in a pack fairly easily. These weigh between two and two and a half pounds with a length of ten to twenty-six inches.

SPLITTING MAUL

As with the forest ax, this is a combination of a hammer, anvil, and ax. These axes have the dullest blades to prevent them from sticking and are meant to cut with the grain. The only thing these are good for is splitting logs, but they do it better than an ax. These can weigh between five and twelve pounds and often have a long handle.

For an ideal survival situation, you would have one of each type of ax since they all do their individual jobs well. However, if you are in a bug out situation, you are likely only going to be able to carry one with you. If you aren't going to use the right tool for the right job, just use extra care. Let's look at another similar option, the tomahawk.

TOMAHAWKS

A good item to consider for your BOB is the survival tomahawk. This reliable tool has evolved rapidly to be a very modern tool. Yet most people aren't too aware of this valuable survival tool. Let's take a look at what it can do for you.

A survival tomahawk has a vast range of utility uses and should be seriously considered by any person preparing for a disaster. A tomahawk is a multi purpose item that can do the job of a variety of tools such as the following:

- ❖ Chopping wood

- ❖ Building entry

- ❖ Glass breaking

- ❖ Vehicle rescue

- ❖ Prying

- ❖ Hunting/butchering

- ❖ Self defense

- ❖ Piercing/cutting sheet metal

- ❖ Opening metal, wood and plastic containers

Not many other tools can do these many practical uses in one compact and simple package. This is why a survival Tomahawk is the most popular tool among some people.

CHOOSING A TOMAHAWK

As with all gear, the first thing to consider when choosing a tomahawk is what you are primarily going to use it for. If you are going to use it mostly for chopping and breaching then you are going to look at a few different features of a tomahawk as your first and primary tool. Let's consider the parts of a tomahawk and determine which styles are best for your individual needs.

HANDLE LENGTH

A tomahawk can range in length from eight to twenty inches. How long your tomahawk should be will depend on what you plan to use it for. A longer handle will give you better leverage for prying and increased force when swinging, but it will be heavier and not as compact. A smaller handle will give you effective usage in close quarters and take up less space in a pack. Consider which type of handle is best suited to which applications.

Long handles are best for:

❖ Splitting wood

❖ Chopping trees

❖ Opening doors

❖ Breaking locks

❖ Butchering large game

❖ Forceful opening of vehicles for rescue

❖ Piercing tough materials

❖ Prying

Short handles are best for:

❖ Long hikes

❖ Close quarters self-defense

❖ Throwing

❖ Precision chopping

❖ Evacuating vehicles

❖ Butchering small game

POLL

The rear of the Tomahawk is known as the poll or butt and is either flat or rounded. A few modern tomahawks also offer the option of a spike on the back. Again, choosing the poll of a tomahawk will depend on what you intend to use it for. A bushcraft tomahawk typically has a flat butt for hammering purposes. A spiked back is good for effective piercing, making it a good tactical tomahawk. Consider the advantages that each option offers:

The flat back is best for the following:

❖ Hammering

❖ Pounding

❖ Forcefully opening doors

❖ Breaking locks

❖ Easier to carry and use

A spike is best for the following:

- ❖ Piercing

- ❖ Prying

- ❖ Self defense

- ❖ Intimidation

CUTTING EDGE

There are many options when it comes to this end of a survival tomahawk. Again we need to look at usage to find the best one for your personal needs.

Length

A longer cutting edge is going to require a larger and heavier ax head. This means added weight, but it will allow you to get greater force behind your swings. This means splitting wood and chopping doors will be easier. Some tactical tomahawks have circular cutouts in their cheeks to save weight without affecting the side of the cutting edge.

This might be a good choice if you want a large cutting edge, but don't want to have too much extra weight in your pack. A narrow cutting edge is often able to pierce deeper since it will have less resistance. This makes it ideal for vehicle extraction and piercing heavy duty materials.

Spine and Beard

It should also be noted that modern tomahawks also have additional sharp edges that aren't on the traditional cutting edge. This can give you a tactical advantage since it opens up additional options for attack and defense. It is worth considering these options if that is something you need in a tomahawk.

While not as many factors to consider as with other bladed tools, there are still a few things to consider when picking a tomahawk for your survival pack. Their high versatility and compact design make them a tool you should definitely consider. Let's move on now to look at multipurpose tools.

MULTIPURPOSE TOOLS

WHEN IT comes to multipurpose survival tools, there are two sets to consider. There are multipurpose tools that serve multiple needs and then there are multipurpose tools that have a variety of gear in one. For example, a duct tape is a multipurpose tool because it has multiple uses and a Multi-Tool is a multipurpose tool because of all the tools it combines together. There are multiple benefits to choosing multipurpose gear.

BENEFITS OF MULTIPURPOSE TOOLS

Perhaps one of the best benefits is that it saves you space. Why pack three items in your BOB when you can pack just one item that does the work of three. When you consolidate items, you will be able to free up space in your BOB for other necessary survival tools such as food or water.

Similarly, a multipurpose tool will save weight. A BOB already calls for you to carry everything but the kitchen sink. Therefore, if you can cut down on the weight, it will make it easier for you to travel long distances when bugging out in a disaster situation.

Lastly, the multipurpose tool will increase simplicity and reduce clutter. If you have more items in a BOB, you are going to find it harder to locate what you need no matter how organized your pack is. When you have less gear, it will be easier to locate what you're looking for.

Let's look at some of the best multipurpose tool options.

SURVIVAL HATCHET

These tools can obviously work as a hatchet, but also can do other jobs such as a pry tool, shovel, and wrench. You can use it in place of high weight to volume ratio steel tools to improve your survival kit.

SURVIVAL WHISTLE

Most people don't think of a whistle as a multipurpose tool. However, this cheap tool can also cover quite a few basics. Most survival whistles come with a compass, dry container and even some kind of fire starting flint.

TARP

There are a lot of things you can do with a tarp. In addition to keeping your gear dry, it can also be used as a shelter. Other uses include signaling and using it as a stretcher.

PLASTIC BAGS

You should pack a few of these in your survival kit since they have many uses. Also, they are lightweight and small. You can use them to carry water, keep clothes and fire starting tools dry, store food and organize small items.

SURVIVAL KNIFE

These tools are covered quite extensively, and this is for a good reason. These are the original multipurpose tool.

DUCT TAPE

Duct tape is another popular multipurpose tool that has been around for awhile. You can use it as an emergency bandage, secure a splint, reinforce clothing, waterproof, rope replacement, shelter building and more.

BANDANA

You can moisten and tie this around your neck to keep cool. It can also be used to filter water, protect you from the sun, be used as a bandage, tie on a splint or replace rope in a task such as a shelter building.

PARACORD

This small and strong cord can be used for shelter building, climbing inclines, setting up a clothes line, fastening a splint or building a snare.

This isn't an all-inclusive list; there are many other multipurpose survival tools that you can choose to help save you space and weight in your BOB. Carefully consider what gear you need and then see if you can find something that serves multiple uses. Next, let's look at the Multi-Tool.

MULTI-TOOLS

Another item that packs a lot of usability into a small package is the Multi-Tool. These can be used for unexpected jobs, solve minor problems of to get your out of a jam with as little hassle as possible. With a lot of Multi-Tools on the market today, it can be difficult to make a good selection. Let's see what you need to know to choose the best Multi-Tools for your survival kit.

A Multi-Tool is an essential piece of gear for any disaster preparer or even a wilderness explorer.

They are a wide range of hand tools that can perform a variety of functions within the simplicity of a single unit. For example, the old-fashioned Swiss Army knife has functions such as a knife, pliers, scissors, bottle opener, screwdriver and more to help you with a variety of tasks. Different Multi-Tools work for different individuals, but all can be helpful when it comes to survival. If you find yourself stranded somewhere, a good Multi-Tool can make all the difference.

As with all the gear we've been discussing you need to keep in mind what you are primarily going to use it for and then choose the best Multi-Tool that fits that need. The first thing you should consider is the type of Multi-Tools.

TYPES OF MULTI-TOOLS

Multi-Tools come in a number of configurations. They can be a simple one piece options or a complex 20-tool large item. In between both of these extremes, you will find a variety of tools to meet any need or desire. Let's look at a few basic styles.

FOLDING MULTI-TOOLS

These are full sized Multi-Tools like the Leatherman and other similar brands. This style is what most people think if when they envision a Multi-Tool. They look like a pair of collapsible pliers with tools that come out of each handle. When not in use both handles swivel up butterfly-style and nestle together around the pliers.

These Multi-Tools offer the greatest number of tools, two of which are often pliers and large scissors. The folding handles often have some type of locking function to prevent accidental closures. These Multi-Tools are often a little big and bulky when carried in a pocket, so they often have a cloth, leather or Kydex Multi-Tool pouch to carry it on your belt.

POCKET MULTI-TOOLS

For some, the belt mounted Multi-Tool is a little too much. A Pocket Multi-Tool is more like a Swiss Army knife and can offer just as many tools, but they are less bulky and don't require special carrying cases. However, most of the tools in a pocket Multi-Tool don't lock into the open position, and there's rarely anything more useful than the scissors or pliers.

SPECIALTY MULTI-TOOLS

These are Multi-Tools that have a very specific application. For example, there are ones specifically designed for firearm maintenance, fishing, and other specific tasks.

TOOL OPTIONS

When it comes to your choices, most Multi-Tools have plenty of options. All Multi-Tools offer the same basics such as a blade, flathead screwdriver and can and bottle opener. Beyond these, the options are pretty much endless. There are Multi-Tools that go so far to offer a small toothpick and tweezers. Larger Multi-Tools will often include a set of large pliers and scissors.

For the purpose of survival, you should look for a Multi-Tool that has carabiners, pocket clips, replaceable tools, vise grips, magnetic drivers and bits or weight-saving measures. Any of these items might help you in a survival situation.

However, as a disaster preparer, you can also keep yourself open to alternate uses for tools. For example, a magnifying glass can be used as a fire starter. Or magnetic screwdrivers can be used to construct a compass. These tools might not be needed every day, but when you do need them, they are there.

All things considered, never assume you'll find the one Multi-Tool that has everything. Expect to have a Multi-Tool for your EDC, another for camping, another for a day on the range and another in your BOB. Each Multi-Tool has its place and can be useful in specific settings.

MAKING A DECISION

It can be quite a challenge to purchase the best Multi-Tool. There is a lot riding on you to make the right choice, and there are plenty of options to choose from as you just learned. When you are looking at all the options before you, there is going to be a lot for you to consider. When choosing a Multi-Tool you want to consider functionality, suitability, and ease of use.

FUNCTIONALITY

The first step is to make sure a Multi-Tool has all the parts and tools you are looking for. There are plenty of cool looking Multi-Tools, but the real question is if they are necessary for your use.

SUITABILITY

All the features and tools aren't going to do you any good if your Multi-Tool selection doesn't actually fit what you want to use it for. You also want to keep in mind how easy it will be for you to carry the Multi-Tool. For example, if you don't wear a belt then it wouldn't do you any good to buy a Multi-Tool with a belt pouch.

Another thing to consider is how easy it is for you to use the Multi-Tool. If you have large hands, you probably don't want to use a small key chain Multi-Tool. On the other hand, you don't want a highly specialized Multi-Tool for general EDC purposes when you could do with a small pocket Multi-Tool.

COMMON MISTAKE WHEN GETTING A MULTI-TOOL

As with a lot of purchases, it can be easy to get led astray with all the options available. You may even be tempted to go online and order your tool without actually handling it first. When it arrives, you might find it too complicated to use, too large or too heavy. Worse you might find it has poor construction and/or materials making it difficult or inconvenient to use.

To avoid this happening to you, take the time to physically try as many tools as possible at a store before making an actual purchase. Go to a hardware store or a sporting goods store, talk with your friends or other disaster preparers and even look at online reviews.

Once you know what Multi-Tool you want you can always purchase online to get a better deal. However, always make sure you purchase from a reputable dealer that has a good return policy in case you aren't satisfied with the Multi-Tool when it arrives.

SPECIAL CONSIDERATIONS WITH A MULTI-TOOL

When purchasing a Multi-Tool you want to keep in mind where you'll be traveling. There are certain cities, towns, and counties that have strict laws or statues about knives. Some restrictions are for blade length, locking mechanisms or carrying methods. You should especially be aware of TSA rules in the event you are traveling.

The last Multi-Tool we want to consider is the smallest of them all, the key chain and wallet Multi-Tool. Let's see how good these options are and whether or not they are right for you.

5 BEST KEY CHAIN AND WALLET MULTI-TOOLS

To adequately prepare for every situation you may realize you need to have small, discreet tools that you can carry with you. This is why key chain and wallet Multi-Tools have become popular since they have a limited impact on your daily routine, some even can pass through airport security. Let's take a look at the top five that you should consider adding to your toolkit.

1. THE POCKETMOD

Having information available in a disaster is just as important as tools. Knowing standard conversions, formulas and even Morse code can make the difference between life and death. However, you aren't always going to have a Smartphone or the internet if you need to look up this information.

The PocketMod is basically a small paper book that you put together yourself, so you always have the information you need. It is made to fit into a standard wallet so you can always have personal information and survival information ready when you need it.

2. TRUE UTILITY KEYTOOL

This is a great key chain Multi-Tool. It comes with the following tools:

- Bottle opener

- Eyeglass screwdriver

- Medium screwdriver

- Large screwdriver

- Nail file

- Thread cutter

- Tweezers

- Fingernail cleaner

What makes this one different from other key chain Multi-Tools is that it fits over a regular key. This means it takes up no extra space if you carry it in your pocket.

3. UTILI-KEY 6-IN-1 TOOL

This is similar to the KeyTool, but it actually looks like a standard key on your key chain.

This one includes the following tools:

➢ Flat screwdriver

➢ Philips screwdriver

➢ Micro-sized screwdriver

➢ Straight blade knife

➢ Serrated blade knife

➢ Bottle opener

This Multi-Tool is compact enough not to interfere with your daily activities but also has enough features that it can help you out in a number of situations. However, this is a Multi-Tool that likely won't pass through airport security.

4. CREDIT CARD SURVIVAL TOOL

This is by far the smallest and most feature packed Multi-Tool. It is no bigger than a credit card and about as thick as two of them.

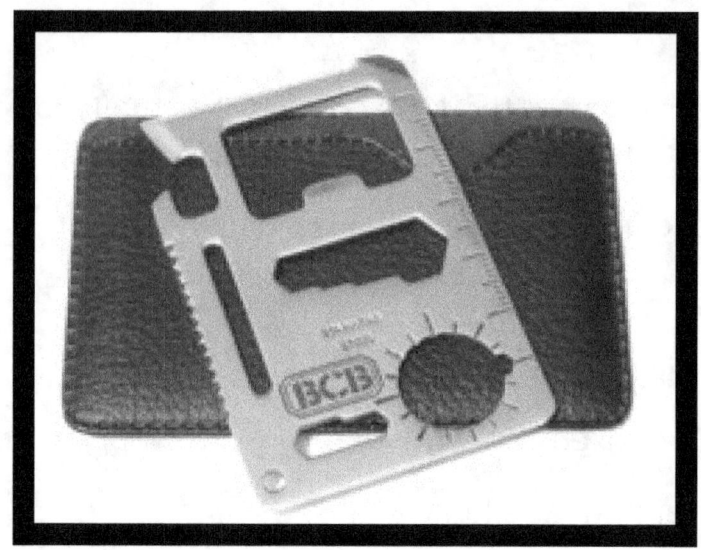

In includes the following tools:

- ➢ Can opener
- ➢ Knife
- ➢ Screwdriver
- ➢ Ruler
- ➢ Cap opener
- ➢ 4 Position wrench
- ➢ Butterfly screw wrench
- ➢ Saw blade
- ➢ Direction ancillary indication
- ➢ 2 Position wrench

If you want everything on a key chain and don't mind dealing with a little extra bulk then consider the EDC Kit. This kit includes five tools that are designed to be more real than compact versions.

This kit includes the following:

➢ Pry bar

➢ 1-inch capsule lighter

➢ Philips head screwdriver

➢ Flat head screwdriver

➢ Precision tweezers

This Multi-Tool weighs less than two ounces, while still being the largest kit on this list.

No matter which of these you choose or if you decide to go with a different Multi-Tool, you will benefit from having survival items with you at all times that can help in a variety of situations. You will be better prepared for any problems that may happen, especially if you can't get to your BOB right away. Now let's consider the important first aid kit and just what you need to handle any emergency in an SHTF situation.

FIRST AID KIT

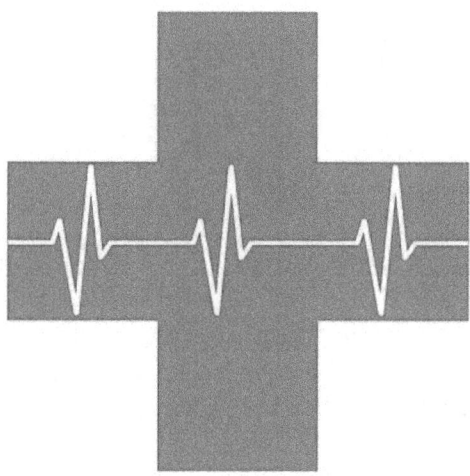

ONE OF THE most essential disaster preparedness items you can have is a first aid kit. All bags and kits you pack should have at least some form of first aid equipment in them. When you have a well-stocked first aid kit, you will be able to treat most injuries and keep moving. However, there is no way you can pack an entire hospital into your disaster kits.

Therefore, as with all the other tools you should assess what injuries are most likely to occur and how you can best treat them while bugging out after an emergency. The best two areas to focus your attention are on trauma and mobility. Let's look at these two areas.

ASSESSING YOUR FIRST AID NEEDS

As I just said, it is important to assess the threats you are likely to be facing when developing a bug out plan or assessing the gear you include in your disaster preparations. When it comes to a first aid kit, you should focus on medium to high probability threats that will have a medium to high impact on you when bugging out after an emergency.

TRAUMA INJURIES

You are certainly going to scrape a knee or cut a hand while bugging out, but these minor injuries are unlikely to affect your moving to safety effectively. This makes them a higher in likelihood but ideally a low impact problem. When planning a bug out first aid kit, you want to address medical emergencies that have a higher level of impact such as trauma injuries. These have a lower probability, but have a higher impact; they could be debilitating to even life threatening.

Trauma injuries can include the following:

❖ Burns

❖ Vehicle collisions

- ❖ Broken bones

- ❖ Arterial bleeding

- ❖ Falls from heights

- ❖ Gunshot wounds

- ❖ Knife wounds

- ❖ Blunt impact injuries

Treating trauma injuries should be one of two focuses for your bug out first aid kit. This will allow you to address the worst problems and keep you alive so you can continue moving when time is critical.

MOBILITY INJURIES

Mobility injuries are those that prevent you from moving efficiently or at your normal pace. They can vary greatly in severity. Most are medium probability and high impact on the risk assessment scale. How a mobility injury affects you is that you will lose your ability to move to a safe location, which is a major issue while bugging out after an emergency.

Mobility injuries can include the following:

- ❖ Blisters

- ❖ Ankle sprains

- ❖ Knee injuries

- ❖ Torn ligaments

- ❖ Frostbite

- ❖ Broken bones

As you can see by this list, mobility injuries cover a wide range of accidents. While some of these aren't life threatening, they can lead to you being unable to evacuate from a dangerous area which can cause further injury or possibly even death. The ability to effectively treat mobility injuries with your first aid kit will help you deal with these injuries and keep you moving to safety.

BUY OR BUILD YOUR FIRST AID KIT

When you add a first aid kit to your BOB, you are faced with two options. You can choose to buy a premade first aid kit from a sporting goods store or online. On the other hand, you can choose to purchase the items you want individually and make your own custom first aid kit. Both choices have their pros and cons; ultimately you will need to choose what is best for you.

PREMADE FIRST AID KITS

This is the easy choice since they come prepacked in a bag that you can simply add to your BOB. However, as with premade BOB, they generally cost more than building your own kits. Also, the quality of the supplies in a premade kit can vary greatly. If you choose to go with a premade kit, then you need to be sure you are getting a quality kit.

Another alternative is to buy a premade first aid kit and then add extra items that you may need like a tourniquet and moleskins.

BUILD A CUSTOM FIRST AID KIT

While this option can be time-consuming there are several advantages to this option including the following:

1. You can choose exactly the items you want, so you don't pay for useless items that don't solve the problems you are likely to face.

2. You have control over the quality of the items.

3. This option is often cheaper since you can shop around for the best price for the best quality first aid items you need.

4. You can get the bag you want by selecting a container that meets your size, features, and quality.

However, there are a seemingly endless number of first aid items on the market. So how can you choose the right items for your first aid kit? Let's look at the most important items you should have in a first-aid kit for disaster preparation.

Blood Clotting Agent - This substance is designed to help with clotting within a wound to stop the bleeding. The military uses these to treat shrapnel and gunshot wounds but has recently been made available for civilian use. These can be used to stop life-threatening blood loss that can occur during a trauma injury in a bug out situation. You can find these in most pharmacy's first-aid isles.

Burn Salve - Burns can occur from many threats when bugging out after an emergency. A burn salve will help provide relief from heat-related injuries, reduce the risk of infection and promote faster healing. These are generally small and lightweight so you can easily fit them into a first aid kit.

Tourniquet - This would be your last line of defense against blood loss. You should use this after other first aid methods for blood loss have failed. Also, tourniquets only work for the arms and legs, but won't help with abdominal or head wounds. It is a better choice to use blood clotting agents, but having a tourniquet can be the difference between life and death in the right situations so it should be included in your first aid kit.

Heavy Gauze - This can be used to apply pressure to wounds, absorb blood and prevent infections. This is a basic first aid item that should be found in any trauma first aid kit. You should pack multiple rolls in a will stocked first aid kit.

Skin Closure Kit - Some recommend having a suture kit to close large wounds or cuts. However, if you don't have any medical training, you will likely do more harm than good when using these. Rather you could pack some Steri Strip Skin Closures for a safe and effective way to close wounds.

Chest Seal - This item helps to create an airtight seal over chest wounds to prevent lung collapse. It is often used for penetrating chest wounds as a result of gunshots, stabbings or shrapnel. These are often sold in pairs to cover the possibility of needed to seal an entry and exit wound.

Trauma Pad - This is a large, sterile dressing that is used to treat large wounds. They are often impregnated with clotting agents to help reduce blood loss. This is perfect for treating trauma injuries in a pre-hospital setting.

MOBILITY ITEMS

Moleskin - The most important maintenance tasks you can do in a bug out situation is to take care of your feet. If you suddenly have to hike for miles in a bug out situation, then you are likely going to develop blisters. Moleskin is designed to provide a cushion around these sore spots to prevent chafing and allow you to safely keep hiking to your bug out destination.

Triangle Bandages - These can be used for a variety of medical purposes including packing wounds, keeping ice bags in place, applying pressure to lacerations, making a sling for an injured arm and trying on splints.

Splint - While you can make a splint out of nearby materials, it is good to have an actual splint. This can also save you time from having to look for splinting materials.

Ace Bandages - These are good for wrapping rolled ankles or twisted knees to give your legs the support you need to keep moving to your bug out location. You can also use them for wound dressing and bandage application.

In addition to trauma and mobility items, you should also have the following general first aid items on hand:

✧ Anti-diarrheal medicine

✧ Medical tape

✧ Pain relievers

✧ EMT shears

✧ Ammonia inhalants

✧ Butterfly strips

✧ Nitrile gloves

✧ Tweezers

✧ Antiseptic wipes

- ✧ Superglue

- ✧ Antibiotics

- ✧ EpiPen

CHOOSING A FIRST AID BAG

When it comes to choosing a bag for your first aid kit you want to choose one that meets your individual needs and has the features you need. It should be compact, functional and accessible.

Perhaps the most important factor in choosing a first aid bag is its size. Whether you are making an individual first aid kit or one for the whole family, the amount of supplies you carry varies, and you will need to find the appropriate sized bag.

As you can see, there are many options when it comes to planning an effective first aid kit. With little organization skill, you will either be able to build your own, buy a premade kit or combine the two approaches. Once you have a first aid kit, you need to review it regularly as a part of your BOB reviews to make sure everything is still usable.

FIRST AID KIT INSPECTION

A first aid kit is an essential part of your BOB. However, a lot of people don't realize the items in a first aid kit are perishable and should be replaced occasionally. No matter what type, size or contents of your first aid kit; you need to inspect it regularly or at least annually. Some items don't have a specific expiration date, so you need to decide when it is appropriate to change out these items. Here are some tips on how you can keep your first aid kit functional.

CONTAINER

The best place to start is the first aid kit container itself. Look for any damage and if there is a zipper whether or not it opens easily. For a plastic or metal container look for cracks, breaks or rust. If there is an o-ring seal, make sure it is still in place and undamaged. When you open the kit, there shouldn't be any foul or unusual odor as a result of mildew.

MEDICATIONS

Medications are the easiest when it comes to knowing when to replace them. Pills, creams, antiseptic wipes, irrigation or eyewash solutions; all of these often have an expiration date on them. If an item is expired, you should replace it.

DRESSING, BANDAGING AND BLEEDING-CONTROL SUPPLIES

These items are the most problematic option. Most kits have both sterile and non-sterile versions. The first step in the inspection process is to separate sterile and non-sterile supplies. Evaluate non-sterile products for the smell of mildew, discoloration or signs of disintegration. If you have any doubt, you should replace the item. The sterile versions require a little more closer inspection.

STERILE GAUZE PADS

These often come in opaque packages. Look at the package for any signs of faded printing, water spots, yellowing or damage. The packaging often has adhesive around the outside edge to seal it closed. If the seal is open or compromised, then the contents are no longer sterile. If the pad is clean and doesn't need to be disposed; you can add it to the non-sterile supplies.

ADHESIVE STRIP BANDAGES

This needs a similar inspection as the sterile gauze pads. However, if the seal or package is compromised or damaged, then the bandage should just be discarded.

ROLLS OF STERILE GAUZE

These are often packaged with clear plastic on one side, sometimes called a "blister" package. As with gauze pads, check the seal and look at the clear side. If there are any yellowing, staining or signs of condensation on the inside of the package, then you should replace the roll. If the seal is compromised, but the role is clean and dry, then you can use it as non-sterile gauze.

ADHESIVE TAPE

This is another item that you need to inspect. If you pick up the tape and the surface without adhesive is slimy, sticky or leaves a residue, then you should replace it. If you don't find any of these issues move on to inspect it for cleanliness, yellowing or damage. You should also check to see if the adhesive is still viable. If the cardboard that the tape is wrapped around is not firm, then it is time to get a new roll.

ELASTIC BANDAGING, STERI STRIPS, BUFFERFLY BANDAGES OR TRIANGULAR BANDAGES

Again inspect for cleanliness, discoloration or damage. If possible, check any adhesive for integrity. Look for rust on safety pins and if they are, replace them.

SCISSORS OR SHEARS

If you notice any signs of rust, corrosion or other defects you should replace them. Use lubricant sparingly to clean any surface rust. Any adhesive tape residue should be cleaned with an appropriate solvent. To confirm sharpness and strength, cut a piece of tape and/or a gauze pad that is folded in double.

LIGHTING GEAR

WE HAVE ALL been stuck in the dark at one point and know how handy a flashlight or other lighting device can be to help us see. For power outages that are short in duration, you can typically get by with an everyday house flashlight. However, for a bug out situation or an extended power out; you should actually have a sturdy flashlight that is sure to navigate you through unfamiliar terrain in the dark. When choosing a flashlight for your BOB, there are a few factors you need to consider.

CHOOSING A FLASHLIGHT

When it comes to choosing a flashlight for your disaster kits, you need to look at a few basic qualities to make the right choice.

LUMENS

Most flashlights list lumens on the packaging or product descriptions. You need to know what this means since it is a great way to compare Flashlights since it involves the basic function of providing illumination. A lumen in the unit of measure for the total amount of visible light produced by a flashlight. In layman's terms, it tells you how bright the flashlight is. The more lumens a flashlight has, the brighter the beam is.

Most basic flashlights are 10 lumens while high-end search and rescue lights can be as high as 18,000 lumens. A typical flashlight for a disaster preparedness kit should be in the 50-100 lumen range, but focus on what you are likely to use your flashlight for when determining how many lumens you actually need.

In general, the following guide will tell you how many lumens you need:

✧ 1-20 Lumens: Finding keyholes, walking in the dark, reading maps.

✧ 20-35 Lumens: General use in the home or garage.

- 35-100 Lumens: General outdoor use, camping, hiking.

- 100+ Lumens: Tactical applications for security guards, police, firefighters.

- 1,000+ Lumens: Search and rescue, caving, extreme outdoor applications.

BULB TYPE

Since flashlight has been invented the light bulb has been the most common bulb. However, in recent years LED flashlights have begun to take over popularity on the market. LED lights are often preferred for EDC kits because they have greater efficiency, better battery consumption, greater brightness and better impact resistance than the regular incandescent light bulbs.

BATTERY TYPE

Many commercial flashlights typically use AA or CR123 batteries. While AA batteries are the most tried and true, the CR123 is more recent. Let's consider each one.

AA BATTERIES

These have been around for years and are a reliable power source for a lot of electronics. AA batteries are based on alkaline cell technology. They are often cheaper and more widely available than newer batteries. Plus they are smaller in diameter and longer in size.

CR123 BATTERIES

These are based on Lithium cell technologies, allowing them to provide greater energy storage and output. This means you get a brighter, longer lasting flashlight. However, these batteries are often more expensive and less readily available. These are shorter in length but are wider in diameter. Flashlight using CR123 batteries are often more compact, but fatter. CR123 batteries are lighter in weight and provide higher performance at cold temperatures.

Determining which battery is best depends on what you are looking for in a flashlight. If you want a flashlight with a battery that is easy to scavenge after a disaster, then you should choose a flashlight based on AA batteries. If you are more concerned about performance and weight, then you should choose a CR123 flashlight.

ALTERNATE POWER CAPABILITY

Batteries are wonderful for a short term power outage and temporary flashlight needs. If you can, it is ideal to have a way to recharge batteries and access to electricity. However, this may not be possible in a post-SHTF situation. As a result, you may want to consider having a flashlight with an alternate power capability.

A hand crank or solar powered flashlight is good for an extended power outage situation especially when your short bug out trip turns into an extended stay in a location without electricity and access to batteries.

SIZE

As with most disaster gear, keeping things as compact as possible is essential. You don't want anything too heavy or bulky. The best flashlights are those that can provide high illumination while staying under four inches long. However, you don't want the smallest possible flashlight since smaller also means it will be less powerful as well.

WEIGHT

Again, size and weight are important factors in your disaster kits. You want the greatest utility at the lowest possible weight. When choosing the best flashlight, you should keep the weight down by selecting a small light or one that is made of lightweight materials like aluminum or titanium. To keep things light, you should choose a flashlight that is less than five ounces.

ADDITIONAL FACTORS

When choosing the best flashlight, you want to consider the basics I mentioned above as well as a few additional factors. First among these is the run time. It is important to know how long a flashlight will operate under continuous use without changing or recharging the battery. Second, since you will be using your flashlight in adverse conditions, you want to consider the water and weather resistance of a flashlight.

WATERPROOF RATING

You never know the conditions under which you are going to have to use your flashlight in an emergency situation. If you happen to need your flashlight in heavy rain or during a flood, then you want a flashlight that is waterproof. Most quality flashlights are rated as waterproof or at least water-resistant. This rating is typically listed as an IPX code.

These would be the following:

✧ IPX-0 - No special protection.

✧ IPX-1 - Protected against falling water. About 3-5mm rainfall per minute for duration of 10 minutes in normal operating position.

✧ IPX-2 - Protected against falling water when tilted at 15 degrees in each direction from the normal operating position.

✧ IPX-3 - Protected against spraying water. Water spraying up to 60 degrees from vertical at 10 liters per minutes at a pressure of 80-100kN/m2 for five minutes.

✧ IPX-4 - Protected against splashing water. Same as IPX-3 but water can be sprayed at all angles.

✧ IPX-5 - Protected against water jets. Water projected at all angles through a 6.3mm nozzle at a flow rate of 12.5 liters per minutes at a pressure of 30kN/m2 for three minutes from a distance of three meters.

✧ IPX-6 - Protected against heavy seas. Water projected at all angles through a 12.5mm nozzle at a flow rate of 100 liters per minute at a pressure of 100kN/m2 for three minutes from a distance of three meters.

✧ IPX-7 - Protected against water immersion for 30 minutes at a depth of one meter.

✧ IPX-8 - Protected against water submersion.

CONSTRUCTION MATERIAL

Flashlights with a metal body construction tend to be tougher. This is important since in a bug out situation a flashlight is going to take a lot of abuse. Selecting a metal flashlight will give you something that lasts longer than other plastic made ones.

BEAM FEATURES

There are few beam features that you need to consider:

Adjustable Beam - When you have an adjustable beam it will increase the versatility of your flashlight. When you can choose to illuminate a wide area for a search and a narrow area for signaling or tactical reasons you will be able to have a flashlight that meets all your needs.

Flashing/Signaling Capabilities - Some flashlights have multiple modes beyond a plain flashlight beam. This isn't a requirement when choosing a disaster flashlight, but it can be a very useful feature. Some flashing programs include the SOS pattern and strobe. Both can help when you need to signal a search party.

When choosing the best flashlight for your disaster kits, you need to consider all of the above along with your personal preferences. Make sure you have a flashlight in all your gear bags. In general, you should store batteries separate since they will corrode if left in the flashlight. Although in a disaster situation you may want to keep your hands free. If this is the case, then you want to consider a headlamp rather than a flashlight.

CHOOSING A HEADLAMP

When it comes to surviving a disaster situation, timing is everything. The time it takes to grab something can make a big difference. Therefore, it can be beneficial to have both hands available. The best way to ensure this at night is to have a headlamp. The headlamp is a convenient and useful tool that can have a number of applications in a survival situation.

However, choosing the right headlamp is always the key.

WHY USE A HEADLAMP?

Consider the various situations you may face after a disaster. Would hands-free illumination help in these situations? Have you ever tried to set up a camp in the dark or tried to find something quickly in low light? In addition to helping light the area around you, LED headlamps can also make great signaling devices; especially if they have a strobe or SOS setting.

Also, a headlamp is less likely to be dropped or lost. Headlamps also provide you a brighter light with a longer battery life. This means you can use a headlamp for several hours a day for over a month before you need to replace the batteries.

WHAT TO CONSIDER

Your priorities differ depending on whether you are looking for hiking, camping, general or disaster headlamp. Often when it comes to choosing a headlamp you want to look at the following:

- ➢ Brightness

- ➢ Distance

- ➢ Battery life

- ➢ Comfort

- ➢ Weight

- ➢ Size

- ➢ IP Rating for water resistance

- ➢ IK Ratings for shock resistance

- ➢ Durability

Some of these topics were already covered above under the segment on flashlights. So I'll refer you back there for those, but in the new areas, we'll discuss them in greater detail.

DISTANCE

If you want visibility in nearly any scenario, then you should choose a headlamp with a combination of floodlight and spotlight settings. A floodlight has the ability to light up a campsite while a spotlight provides a focused beam that can pinpoint a distant object.

BALANCING COMFORT AND SIZE

Similar to your BOB, you want to choose a headlamp that is both comfortable and lightweight while also being appropriate to guide you through your night travels.

COMFORT

If you are going to wear a headlamp for extended periods of time or while doing activities, then a top strap can be a good option since it gives added stability. Whether you have a top strap or not; you should adjust the band so that it fits snugly enough to keep the light in place while shaking your head. To eliminate neck strain, choose a headlamp that also has an adjustable light angle.

WEIGHT

The number of lights and type of battery will influence the weight of a headlamp. You should choose a model that meets your needs while has a reasonable weight that you can support for a long time.

SIZE

The more LEDs, the brighter your headlamp. However, with each additional LED you are adding to the size and weight of a headlamp and increasing battery drain. Depending on your needs, determine the best size and number of LEDs that you need in balance with a headlamp that isn't too heavy or depletes the batteries too quickly.

In the flashlight segment above we discussed waterproof ratings. However, there is also an IK Rating that refers to mechanical impact and measures how many joules of downward force an object can withstand. Consumer products typically have resistance ratings given in meters. This indicates the height at which the items can be dropped from and still survive the impact.

A reliable and good quality headlamp can make an excellent addition to your emergency kit. Using the above guide you will be able to choose the best headlamp for your needs. Lastly, let's take a look at generators.

GENERATORS

When disaster strikes, you certainly aren't going to lug a generator with you to your bug out location. However, if you are already going to have a bug out location set up in advance, then you should have a generator in place as an alternative power source. Let's take a look at what you need to consider when choosing a generator.

Wattage is very important when choosing a generator since this will determine how much you can support. Smaller wattage means you will most likely only be able to care for the bare minimum, which may not work for a long term power loss situation. Here is a great wattage guide that you can view here:

http://tinyurl.com/j23b2bn

RUNTIME

Once you've determined how much wattage you need, you next want to consider runtime. This is defined as the amount of time a generator can run with a full fuel tank. If you simply want to keep the light on after a power outage, then runtime is very important. However, if you need a high-grade source of power, then runtime isn't as important as other features such as capacity, weight or noise.

FUEL TYPE

Most people are unaware that generators can come in various fuel types. In addition to gas, some generators run on propane or natural gas. There are even some powered by sunlight. Fuel type is important since you want to choose one that is available in bulk after an emergency or safe to store before an emergency. You also want to consider the shelf life of the fuel.

FOUR TYPES OF GENERATORS

STANDBY GENERATOR

This is the most basic and common type of generator. They automatically turn on and take over when a power failure occurs and continue until power is restored. These are heavy duty and typically run on gas, diesel, propane or natural gas. Standby generators are often expensive and not very portable but are excellent at powering your bug in a and bug out location.

PORTABLE GENERATOR

This option likely won't have as much wattage as the heavy duty standby generator but gives you the benefit of being more portable in case you need to move. However, they won't have the staying power or wattage of a standby generator.

SOLAR POWER GENERATOR

Unless you spend a lot of money on solar panels, a solar power generator won't be practical for heavy duty power needs. If you don't have fuel, then a solar powered generator will be handy to operate smaller electronics. There are a few heavy duty solar powered generators that can power one or two higher grade power needs, but the technology, in general, isn't ready to meet the major power needs of an entire home. Perhaps the biggest benefit of solar powered generators is their totally silent operation.

These are similar to portable generators with just a few exceptions. In addition to being more lightweight, they are also quieter than a portable generator.

With so many generators to choose from, it can be a bit overwhelming to choose a generator. However, keeping in mind what you need a generator for and using the above information you will be able to choose an appropriate generator.

Now that we've looked at some of the most important disaster gear let's now take a look at few extra items that you may want to include in your BOB.

OTHER BOB GEAR

BIVY BAGS

THE BIVY bag offers an added versatility to your bug out experience. It allows you to stay in a limited space that would otherwise be unable to fit a tent. Also, they are light and fast to set up, plus they can be packed easily for any extreme situation that may arise. These can fit in your BOB and your car emergency kit for any survival situation.

Survival blankets are awkward, bulky and in some ways can be inefficient. On the other hand, Bivy bags are a multi-use, reusable and life-saving item that you can sometimes get for under $10. Bivy bags take the form of a body which makes them less bulky and more efficient at keeping you warm.

WHAT ARE BIVY BAGS?

A Bivy or bivouac sack is a waterproof and windproof layer used to seal your sleeping system instead of using a tent. Bivy bags are used by many people who want a simpler form of light travel or during an emergency. You simply slip it over your sleeping bag or ground pad to get protection from wind chill, rain, and other winter conditions while also adding five to ten degree Celsius in insulation.

Basically they are a single wall tent that was originally designed for mountaineers and climbers who needed lightweight protection during emergencies. After years of modifications and added specs, a Bivy bag can now be used for a variety of emergency situations.

BIVY SHELTER VS. BIVY BAG

The types can vary between sacks to shelters. The shelters are a small, low-rise tent that is often constructed with hoops or poles that lift the fabric above you so you can have a little sit-up space. The Bivy bag may feel claustrophobic or confined for some, but the Bivy shelter can give you more space to move around, without the weight of a tent.

CHOOSING A BIVOUAC SYSTEM

Most bivouac systems are made from material similar to that of a tent, urethane coated nylon on top of a rip stop nylon layer treated with a waterproof laminate such as GoreTex. This allows some humidity and condensation to pass through while still protecting against the majority of water from the outside.

Consider what you plan to use your system for. If is for winter camping, survival situations, backpacking or an outdoor sleeping system? What type of sleeping conditions do you need? For example, are you a light sleeper who needs more room to sleep?

FOUR-SEASON SYSTEM

This option is sturdy, waterproof and roomy while also being lightweight and packable. These Bivy bags are often made with an added pole to make more room inside the bag while still being durable enough for the extreme weather. While they may add a little more weight to your BOB, they are still lighter than a tent and will keep you comfortable even under the most severe of weather conditions.

When choosing a Bivy bag, consider what you are going to be using it for and what type of conditions you'll be facing. Insects, thunderstorms, wind, snow and heat all play a role in determining what type of Bivy bag you'll pack in your BOB.

Another important item that you may need to pack in your BOB depending on where you live is rain gear. Let's consider what you need to know before packing these items in your BOB.

RAIN GEAR

SHTF situations don't only occur during best weather conditions. You're going to need to be prepared for all weather conditions, including rain. Rain can spell real trouble, especially when it's cold out; hypothermia can occur which can lead to death. Even when hypothermia isn't a concern, it still isn't fun to walk around completely wet.

If you need to leave your home in a bug out situation, then you need to be prepared for whatever weather you may face. This means to have good solid rain gear that will help keep your warm and dry. You also want to have a backup plan in place in case you don't have access to your primary rain gear. Let's consider what you need to have in rain gear as well as the alternatives in case you can't access your rain gear.

CHOOSING QUALITY GEAR

You should have your quality rain gear purchased and packed in your BOB. You want to choose items that will keep your entire body warm and dry. You never know what time of year you are going to have to bug out and how cold or wet the weather may get before you can get to shelter. The first step in getting quality rain gear is to make sure you have the right material.

When it's raining, the material your rain gear is made from is critical to your comfort and warmth. When it comes to protecting yourself from rain, there are two rules you need to be aware of. First, you want to remain dry and warm. Second, you want to stay warm if you can't stay dry. To do this, the most important thing is to stay away from cotton. While many feel cotton is a nice, natural and breathable fabric; it will not keep you warm when it becomes wet.

When it comes to choosing natural materials for your BOB, you want to use wool. Wool is a wonderful material since it will insulate you and keep you warm even when wet. Thanks to modern technology there are even wool materials that are lightweight and non-scratchy.

In addition to wool, you can also use synthetic materials. These materials help to wick moisture away from the skin. This allows you to stay warm and dry.

You won't find a single jacket rain gear that works for all situations. You should look for a quality outer shell and then layer up with wool and light jackets underneath. The best material for a waterproof shell is Gore-Tex. This technology keeps water out, but also allows your body to breathe so you won't have condensation build up inside your rain gear.

COVER EVERYTHING

When it comes to choosing rain gear, you want to consider more clothing than just a jacket. You want to have everything fully covered from your head down to your toes. Let's consider what else you need besides a jacket.

HEAD COVERING

Again, hypothermia is your main concern, and it is more likely to occur when you're wet. In addition to a hooded jacket, you should consider getting a hat for extra protection. If your body is well-insulated, but the head is exposed your core body temperature can drop quickly because the scalp has a lot of blood vessels that cool down when exposed to the cold.

This cooled blood is then circulated back into the body, causing your core to cool down quicker. It is good to have a winter hat or balaclava made from wool or synthetic materials to keep you warm in the cold and wet.

TORSO

This is where your jacket matters. As we already said, there isn't one jacket that is perfect for all weather condition. This is why you want to spend your money on a quality outer shell that can protect you from the wind and rain while you can put additional layers underneath as needed. Wearing layers will insulate the body better than a single thick layer.

Again, you want to make sure it is made out of synthetic, waterproof and windproof materials. You need to be careful when choosing a shell that meets your needs since not all jackets are made the same. You can identify the difference by keeping in mind the following terms.

Water Resistant - This material offers you the least protection against rain. It will resist water penetration, but not completely and not for long. Over time, water will seep in, and you are going to get wet.

Water-Repellant - This material is a step up from the previous. Water can't easily get through this material, but eventually, will. Even if the material surface is covered with a waterproof coating, it isn't guaranteed that no water will get inside.

Waterproof - This is a jacket that is completely sealed against water penetration. You will stay dry with this option.

The important thing to remember when buying a shell to keep warm and dry is that you want to spend a little extra to ensure a higher quality jacket. Higher priced jackets are often made with materials that keep you dry, but also provide breathability for your body.

LEGS

During rainy weather, you also want to keep your legs dry. Rain pants are often sold with rain jackets. Even if they don't come as a set, you can buy a separate set of rain pants. The same material requirements as the jacket apply for the pants. Rain pants should be high quality, waterproof and breathable. You should also wear pants or leggings underneath that are wool or synthetic material to wick away moisture.

FEET

Cold and wet feet will certainly make you feel miserable. When it comes to surviving in a bug out situation, it is very important to maintain warm and dry feet. To do this, you need good socks, preferably wool or Gore-Tex. Good socks keep your feet warm even when they're wet.

Combine this with a good set of boots, and you're all set. You can even choose to layer your socks when you're in a very cold environment. You can choose to wear rain boots, but these can be difficult to walk in when bugging out after a disaster. Rather it is best to have a good pair of waterproof hiking boots. Always remember to wear-in your boots before you need them for an emergency.

RAIN GEAR ALTERNATIVES

Whether you have rain gear packed in your BOB or not, there are some extras you need to have on hand as well. There are a few other items you should have packed.

PONCHO

This is a smart thing to pack. It gives you an added layer of protection that works for both you and your pack. You can never have too many layers of protection against the rain. In addition, if you don't wear your poncho it can double as a tarp, and they are very light weight.

TARP

You should also have a tarp or two in your BOB. In the event you are without any other rain gear, you can cut a hole in your tarp and wear it as a poncho. The tarp is also excellent for building a makeshift shelter or to keep your gear covered and dry in a heavy rainstorm.

GAITERS

These are another handy item to have packed in your BOB. You can get a version made from Gore-Tex that you strap underneath your boot to help cover your ankle and lower leg. These act to secure the opening at the top of your boot to give an added layer of waterproofing protection for your lower leg and feet.

GOGGLES

When it is raining really hard, you could choose to wear goggles in order to keep the rain out of your eyes. It will also help increase your visibility.

GARBAGE BAGS

You can never pack too many garbage bags in your BOB. They have many uses, and you can even use one as a backup poncho. Just cut a hole or rip the middle of the bottom seam of the bag and then you can wear it as a poncho. You can also use it to wrap your pack or other belongings.

When you have good clothes worn in layers that dry quickly, however, you should always make sure you pack a spare set of clothes in Ziploc bags so if you do get wet and stop moving you have dry clothes to change into.

It is also important to keep your rain gear clean. Even if something is waterproof like Gore-Tex, it won't function at peak levels if it is dirty. Lastly, don't try to pack an umbrella. These are both impractical and bulky. You can have one stored in your vehicle, but you shouldn't have one in your BOB.

Next, let's consider the gas mask and how you can make sure you make the right choice for one that protects you from potential chemical disasters.

GAS MASKS

With the threat of chemical attacks these days, many are questioning whether they should buy gas masks as a part of their BOB. Let's look at what you need to know about gas masks and how you can pick the right one for your needs. Consider the following before you choose to buy a gas mask.

DON'T BUY SURPLUS

You have likely seen most gas mask advertisements in surplus ads online or in catalogs. Most of these are a good deal only because they are outdated and have been replaced by more effective models; sometimes they may even be defective. Even if they still work, a lot of older masks are known for being difficult to deploy and ill-fitting even if you correctly strap them on according to instructions.

There is never a guarantee on a domestic or imported surplus mask because most come with expired filters. If you want a gas mask for your BOB, you certainly don't want to buy surplus, no matter how good the savings seems.

When buying a gas mask, there are certain criteria that you need to consider. First, you want to make sure both the mask and filter are rated for chemical blowing and riot control agents. This is designated by the CBA/RCA rating. The NBC rating determines protection against nuclear, biological and chemical agents.

There are some gas masks on the market that are no better than a surgical mask. While this may work for most biological threats, it is important to have a mask and filter rated for nuclear and chemical threats as well in the event of an SHTF scenario. Before ordering from any supplier be sure to discuss this with them. It is preferred that you buy from a company that does third party testing.

Another part is the filter connections. The best are with connections on both sides rather that just one side or in the front. This provides you greater flexibility and allows you to positively attach a replacement on the opposite port before removing an expired one.

Lastly, the field of view is something you should consider. You want an unobstructed view during times that you have to use a gas mask. A lot of surpluses and older gas masks have a small goggle-type eye hole. This will take away nearly all of your peripheral vision. If you have prescription glasses, you certainly want to make sure the gas mask fits appropriately while you're wearing your glasses.

EXTRA FILTERS

Gas mask filters have an expiration date, and they certainly don't last as long as you think. Most filters need to be replaced after several hours of use depending on your environment and the gas concentrations. Even when breathing normal air, they should be replaced every 24 hours.

This shows you just how many extra filters you are likely to need in the event of a disaster. You also want to keep track of the expiration date of filters on hand in your storage. Filters can be expensive, and the cost can add up so choose carefully.

GAS MASK STORAGE

A gas mask is only effective if you have securely deployed it before an attack. Once an attack happens it is often too late. This is especially true when it comes to chemical and biological agents where even a momentary exposure can prove fatal. So where should you store your gas mask? Are you going to need one at home, work, and in your car? It is impossible to determine when a disaster may strike. Even if you own a gas mask, a sudden and unexpected attack may not provide you with enough time to effectively deploy your gas mask.

Deploying and strapping on a gas mask isn't nearly as easy as TV and movies have made it seem. Many deaths have occurred from incorrectly strapping on a gas mask or not even being able to put it on during stress and panic. There are even accounts of people suffocating to death because they don't remove the plastic seal before putting on new filters. This is why the military holds gas-mask training exercises. You need practice to properly fit and use a gas mask. It is best to get hands-on training by a professional and then practice at home on a regular basis.

When it comes to gas masks, remember they are only a temporary defense. You can't wear a gas mask indefinitely. So you should have a permanently protected place to go to in an SHTF scenario. However, if you're going to need a gas mask for temporary use then consider the following types of gas masks and their pros and cons.

GAS MASK OPTIONS

OLD SOVIET SERIES OF MASKS

This is likely the most common mask in the world today. These are an inexpensive and relatively simple to use option. You can find them in several sizes and are good for those who only have minimal gas mask training.

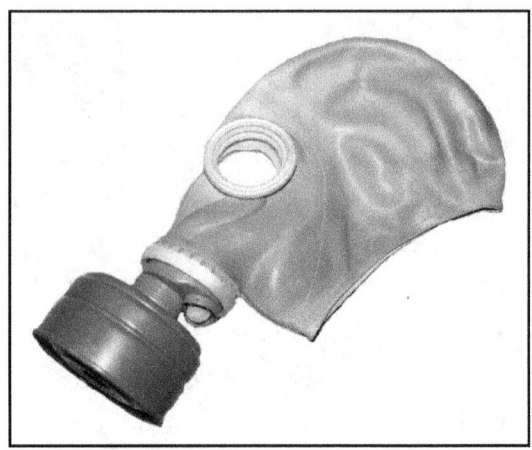

Pros:

✧ Easy to use

✧ Good to very good protection

✧ Easy to change filters

Cons:

✧ No voicemitter so difficult to understand

✧ Lens's will fog up if not kept clean

ISRAELI MASKS

This is the next most popular gas mask. It is a little more expensive, but it also very good. Let's look at the pros and cons.

Pros:

✧ Large eye lenses

✧ Nose cup prevents fogging under nearly all conditions

✧ Easy to change filters

✧ Has a voicemitter, making communication easier

Cons:

✧ It is easy to over tighten, cutting off blood flow to the scalp causing a headache

✧ Needs a hood for proper head protection

AMERICAN MASKS

The basic model here is the M-17 series that is used by US forces and copied by the Czech and other forces. These masks vary greatly in cost, from cheap to very expensive. It all depends on where they were made. Most masks in this series have been well tested.

Pros:

✧ Large eye lenses

✧ Nose cup to prevent fogging and draws air across the eyes to clear them

✧ Voicemitter for communication

✧ Many accessories

Cons:

✧ Easy to over tighten

✧ Requires hood for complete head protection

✧ Filters are difficult to change

When it comes to choosing a gas mask, it is an eleven step process:

1. Choose a gas mask that is currently used by the modern military, ideally NATO countries. This ensures quality, standards, and filter interchangeability.

2. Never use an outdated or surplus gas mask. For example, don't get an M9 US gas mask when you should be getting an M17 US gas mask.

3. Always check the size to make sure it properly fits you.

4. Check the air tightness before purchasing. Put on the gas mask, check the fit, unscrew the filter, cover the filter hole with your palm and inhale. If air comes in, then don't buy the mask.

5. Look for mechanical faults. Is it scratched, torn or has any cracks in the goggles? Don't buy it.

6. Make sure the gas mask comes with a drinking cord and that it fits airtight. When you have the mask on, pinch the end of the drinking cord and try to suck.

7. Check all the valves since they are the most important part of the mask. They should be elastic, clean and have no tears or cracks. Also, make sure the mask you are purchasing comes with extra valves.

8. Look into a specialized flask for the drinking cord and test it.

9. Make sure you get spare filters that can protect you from military grade chemical agents. If there are industrial complexes in your area, you may also want to consider a mask that protects you from industrial chemicals as well.

10. All filters, both the main and spare ones should be vacuum packed. The seals shouldn't be broken, and you should only take them out of their packaging for training purposes.

11. Make sure it is easy to breathe and see in your gas mask.

Now you know what to look for when purchasing a gas mask. Another area of gear that you need to consider is whether or not you want to carry a self-defense weapon and if so what type works best for you.

SURVIVAL SELF DEFENSE WEAPONS

HUMANS HAVE a natural instinct to be protective; they want to protect themselves, their homes and their family. A part of this personal and home defense is determining whether or not you want to own a firearm or other self-defense weapon for using when bugging in or out after an emergency situation.

There are many pros and cons when it comes to buying a firearm as well as having it in your home for an emergency. Each person first needs to consider why they want a firearm and what they plan to use it for.

The average disaster preparer will have firearms for both self-defense and survival. Firearms have proven to be most effective for survival. However, there are individuals who don't want to use a gun; even in a survival situation.

Common sense also tells us that we shouldn't rely on just one type of tool or weapon should it break, become lost or otherwise unusable or un-accessible. The good news is, there are many other ways that you can protect yourself and your home if you don't want to use a firearm. Think of the following tools as additional ways to provide for your self-defense.

EDGED WEAPONS

One of the first choices aside from a firearm is to use a bladed or edged weapon. This can range from pocket knives up to samurai swords. There is a never ending array of blades to choose from. Some are specifically designed to help with self-defense while others aren't designed for that but can still serve the same purpose if needed. Knives work well in tight quarters but do require you to get close to your assailant.

If you are going to choose a knife, make sure it is sturdy and strong. See our chapters on choosing the best knives for your needs.

BLUNT OBJECTS

These can be effective self-defense weapons depending on what you're using. They are also easily found, and I am sure you probably have multiple around the house already. Just take a look in your garage or workshop; there are screwdrivers, hammers, sledgehammers and even small pieces of lumber that you can use as for self-defense in a pinch. Other options around your home include the baseball bat, crowbar, metal pipe and other sturdy objects.

Obviously, some blunt objects aren't going to be efficient long-term self-defense weapons, but knowing what you can use and practice is important.

When you know what to grab can save seconds and possibly your life.

DOGS

When the power goes out, most alarms aren't going to work. Dogs are an effective alarm system for home and can even be a defensive weapon depending on the breed. Even a small dog can make a good defensive option and alert you when something is happening. Larger breeds that are bred specifically for protection purposes can serve as both an alarm and attack intruders. Just remember if you are going to use a dog for protection you want to train them properly.

CHEMICAL SPRAYS

There are plenty of these for a variety of situations; bear spray, pepper spray, and mace. While these options may not stop someone, they will give you the upper hand and allow you to prepare yourself for a better defense. Also, spraying a human with something designed for grizzly bears is likely to incapacitate them. Chemical sprays have the added benefit of being kept easily on your body and stashed around the home.

It is important to keep in mind that these sprays can also harm you, especially if you are close to the person you are spraying. Foam sprays are slightly safer since they can't mist backward. This is important especially if you are moving around quickly.

Don't forget that you aren't limited just tools and weapons, but you can also train yourself in self-defense. It can be a good idea to receive specialized self-defense training. If you don't have time to grab a self-defense weapon, then it is a good idea to know how to use your own body to disarm or incapacitate someone.

Once you decide to purchase a self-defense weapon, you need to consider several factors. When it comes to firearms, you need to be aware of the different types of guns.

Most people prefer the pistol for home defense since they are accurate and easy to shoot. However, they are also complicated and can be difficult to operate when you are under severe stress. Pistols also aren't as reliable as revolvers. Long guns are extremely effective and can also be used for hunting. However, they aren't as portable and can even be difficult in emergency situations since they require both hands to operate.

When purchasing a firearm, you need to have some basic understanding and knowledge to make the proper buying decision. It is important to also consider your purpose before choosing a firearm. Self-defense, hunting, target shooting or even skeet shooting all require a different type of firearm to meet each specialized needs. You also need to consider the size and your budget.

For firearms, you also want to consider caliber and ammunition. People most commonly use .45, .357 and .9 mm ammunition. These numbers refer to the bore size or diameter of the firearm barrel. Often the larger the caliber, the greater the stopping power of the bullets. For home and self-defense, it makes sense to get a higher caliber since you want to stop someone as soon as possible to prevent them from hurting you or your family. However, it also means the weapon is going to have greater recoil; making it harder to shoot accurately.

This leads us into considering the size and comfort of a firearm. This will have an influence on how you use it and where you store it. You should practice shooting various guns so you can see which one is most comfortable for you to operate.

Keep in mind where you plan to store your firearm safely. Some people prefer a handgun that they can keep with themselves in a holster. Others what to keep their firearms locked in a safe at home. If this is the case, make sure you can access it quickly and efficiently in an emergency.

These tips can help you to find the best firearm for your needs. However, what works for one person may not work for others. So if a firearm isn't for you, let's look at some non-conventional self-defense options. Let's start with the tactical pen.

TACTICAL PEN

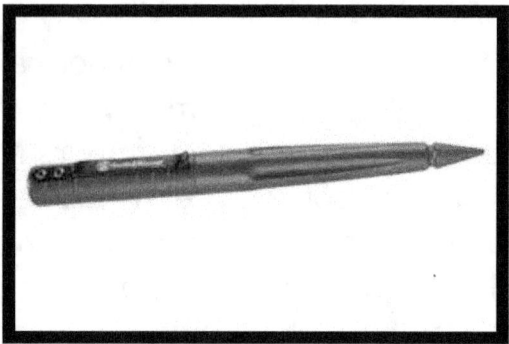

This can be a good self-defense option in an emergency. They can be an excellent option for EDC kits since they are small in size, lightweight, easily concealable and have dual purpose function. Let's take a look at what these are and how you can choose a good one for your EDC kit.

WHAT IS A TACTICAL PEN?

Basically, a tactical pen is a writing implement that can also be used as a defensive weapon. They are typically made from metal or very strong plastic. The best tactical pens are those made from aircraft grade aluminum or titanium since they make a strong, lightweight tactical pen. One or both ends of the pen are often tapered to a point so it can be used as a thrusting self-defense tool. A normal pen would bend or break under self-defense condition, but a tactical pen is designed specifically for these situations.

There are many reasons you should consider carrying a tactical pen. For some, it is as simple as wanting a high-quality pen that looks good and matches the other gear in their EDC kit such as the folding knife and other tactical equipment.

However, for the majority of people, they carry a tactical pen because they want a reliable self-defense tool that can be easily hidden in plain sight. A knife or firearm can easily draw attention, but a tactical pen is more of a gray man option. Most tactical pens will also pass security or TSA inspection so you can literally carry them anywhere. With basic training, tactical pen users can protect themselves wherever they are.

There are also many tactical pens that are designed as a non-lethal weapon with a blunt end. These are meant to apply painful force to pressure points, sensitive areas and vulnerable locations on the body of an attacker. This can be an appealing option for those who don't want a lethal self-defense option but still want to protect themselves from an attacker.

Lastly, there are those who want to reduce the weight of their EDC kit by combining a self-defense tool with a writing implement. If you want a powerful self-defense tool that is concealable and compact, consider the following when choosing your own tactical pen.

QUALITY

When it comes to choosing a tactical pen, the first thing you want is to choose one that writes well. This is the basic function of a pen and is what you are going to be using it for 99% of the time you have it. You should choose a tactical pen that can accept ink refills from a number of quality producers.

FEATURES

After you have a good writing pen, you should start looking at the defense features to choose the best tactical pen for your needs. First, decide how you are going to use your tactical pen as a self-defense tool. For example, a smaller woman is going to struggle with a blunt ended tactical pen and might want to choose a sharper one. On the other hand, a larger person could probably use enough force with a blunt ended pen.

GRIP

The pen should be comfortable in your hand for both writing and when using it as a self-defense tool. If you are swinging with any velocity, you want to make sure the pen is going to stay in your hand upon impact. Therefore, the best tactical pen should have ridges or grooves for your fingers so you can have better grip retention.

ATTACHMENT CLIP

The best tactical pens also should have a good pocket clip that allows you to attach it to a pocket, bag or belt. Some pens will even have additional attachment options for things like key rings, carabiners, and paracord. You should make sure the tactical pen you choose is one that has an attachment option that fits with how you intend to carry your pen.

HOW TO USE A TACTICAL PEN

There are many ways that you can choose to deploy a tactical pen for the purpose of self-defense. If you are going to carry a tactical pen, you should train in how to use it effectively. Even after you learn proper techniques, you should practice regularly. This way, should you ever need to actually use the pen for self-defense it will be muscle memory and an automatic reaction.

Some typical pressure points to use the tactical pen on includes the following:

➢ Armpit

➢ Neck

➢ Inner arm

➢ Inner thigh

Also, the tactical pen can be used on the following sensitive areas:

- ➤ Throat

- ➤ Eyes

- ➤ Ears

- ➤ Groin

- ➤ Ribs

- ➤ Solar Plexus

- ➤ Nose

As you can see, there are plenty of options that make carrying a tactical pen a good option. They are reliable and multipurpose. Using the above suggestions you will be able to find a good tactical pen for your EDC kit. Next, we'll look at another good self-defense alternative; the slingshot.

SLINGSHOT

Often when people hear the word slingshot, they envision a mischievous child. However, slingshots have evolved over the years and now play a vital role in survival scenarios. Let's take a look at how you can use a slingshot as a survival tool and what to look for when choosing one for your BOB.

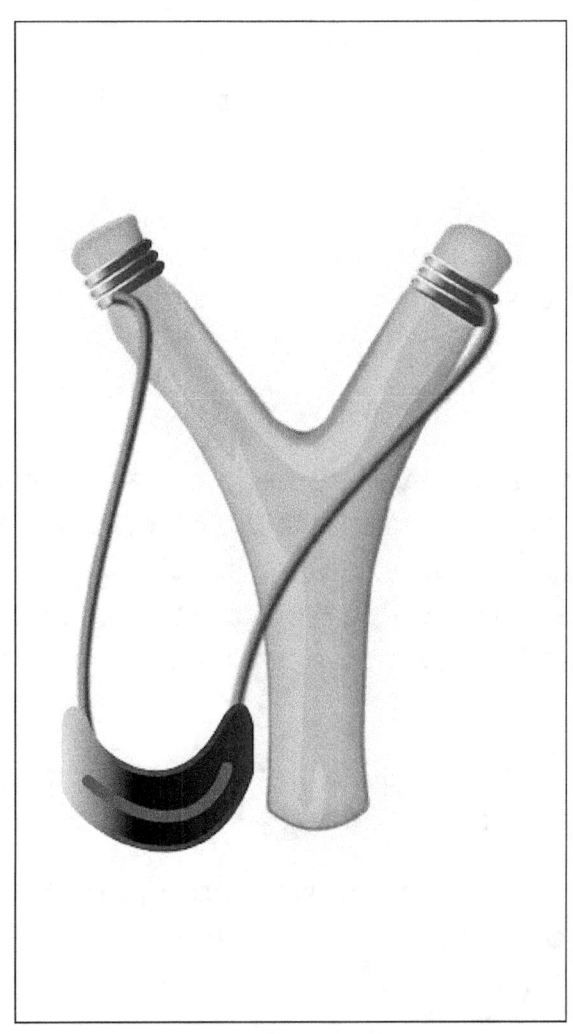

SHOULD YOU GET A SLINGSHOT?

Slingshots are a great addition to any BOB because they are lightweight and versatile, plus you don't have to worry about packing additional ammo. Whether you find yourself in an urban or wilderness survival situation after a disaster, a slingshot can use projectiles from pretty much anything around you.

This also means less weight in your BOB, and you'll never have to worry about running out of ammo.

SLINGSHOT USES

Slingshots can be used for two main purposes: hunting and self-defense. This makes it one of the more versatile survival tools.

HUNTING

Those who have never hunted with a slingshot as a weapon may think this isn't possible. However, a slingshot can be an excellent hunting weapon by killing most small game from thirty feet away. Consider some advantages to using a slingshot for hunting:

1. You give off a smaller profile, making it harder for animals to spot the danger.

2. It allows you to maneuver through brush easier allowing you to improve your shot or conceal yourself easier.

3. It is truly a silent weapon that won't give away your location to animals or unfriendly humans.

Also, a slingshot can be easily modified to shoot arrows if you need to hunt larger game. It can even be modified to use as a form of bow fishing. This often involves adding a reel to the slingshot.

As with hunting, you shouldn't discount the use of a slingshot as a self-defense weapon. They can be used against both animals and humans. Consider some of the benefits of using a slingshot as a self-defense weapon:

1. The small size allows you to conceal it easily.

2. Just showing it and making it known you aren't unarmed can prove to an attacker that you won't be an easy target.

3. You can easily find ammo all around you, so it works for long-term survival situations.

4. You don't need to worry about keeping it dry.

5. It is completely silent so you can take down targets with stealth and not alert anyone else nearby.

WHAT TO LOOK FOR WHEN CHOOSING A SLINGSHOT

If you've used a slingshot before, then you know how valuable they can be as a survival weapon. However, what most don't realize is that not all slingshots are created equal. There are some distinct features of slingshots that make some better suited to survival than others. Let's consider the different features you need to consider when choosing a slingshot for survival purposes.

Most slingshots are made from one of three materials: metal, wood, and plastic. Let's consider the pros and cons of each along with key considerations to help you determine which frame material is best for your slingshot needs.

Metal

✧ Light and strong

✧ Most expensive, but sturdier and last longer

✧ For a BOB, the ideal choice is an aluminum or steel slingshot with a plastic or ergonomic foam handle

Wood

✧ A classic design

✧ Often engineered in a simple Y-shape with a rubber band attach to each fork

Plastic

✧ Plastics differ and can have different qualities

✧ Often the most economical

✧ Modern plastics like glass filled nylon provide durability and weight

Modern slingshots have two types of bands: flat bands and rubber tubing. Determining the best for your needs depends on what you intend to use it for. Tubing is often better for hunting since it is more durable. Flat bands provide greater accuracy and work better as a self-defense weapon. Let's consider the benefits of both.

Rubber

✧ Last long so they make a better choice for hunting if you need to use them over an extended period of time.

✧ There are many types of rubber tubes that can be chosen to meet any desired draw weight.

Flat Bands

✧ Make it easier to draw and often produce faster projectiles. If you aren't going to be firing a lot, but want improved accuracy, then this is a better option.

✧ Faster and more accurate than a rubber tubing because of the rapid snap back speed.

Both rubber tubing and flat bands are cheap. It may be a good idea to experiment with both options to see which suits you the best.

OTHER FEATURES

The best slingshots will offer you features that make them different from a standard slingshot. Some of these features are good for survival or hunting while others aren't. Let's consider the additional features that are important to you.

GRIP

✧ No matter how you intend to use your slingshot, you want to have a comfortable grip.

✧ When you have a good grip, you will be able to fire more shots and increase your accuracy without added hand and wrist fatigue.

✧ The best slingshots are those that have a contoured handle to naturally fit your hand.

SIGHT

✧ This can help improve the accuracy of your shots.

✧ This is great for those with little experience since it reduces your practice time to improve accuracy.

✧ Sight is important if you are going to be aiming at lots of small targets.

✧ A sight is less needed if you are going to be using it for larger targets and in shorter distances.

✧ The best hunting slingshots often have a sight attached.

✧ Many slingshots have a screw-cap hollow handle where you can store things such as spare tubing or ammunition.

✧ Although not a necessary feature, a hollow handle can be handy to pack other survival gear into the handle.

A slingshot is a versatile tool for all individuals and it a good option for those who don't like the idea of firearms but don't have the strength and size to use hand weapons. However, as with all weapons, it is important to practice regularly to become proficient in the use of a slingshot.

Lastly, let's take a look at your vehicle. What do you need to look for in a good bug out vehicle and how can you upgrade your current vehicle?

BUG OUT VEHICLE

IF YOU ARE planning to bug out after an emergency and need to travel long distances, then you may want to consider getting a good bug out vehicle. A bug out vehicle is something more than a vehicle that would just get you from Point A to Point B. You might need to sleep in it, cook in it and possibly live through some of the most dangerous moments of your life. Let's take a look at points you need to keep in mind when it comes to choosing a bug out vehicle option that will help you overcome all the challenges of bugging out after an emergency.

The best bug out vehicle will vary depending on the person and their circumstances. Let's look at each of these points individually to see how you can choose and incorporate a bug out vehicle into your emergency bug out plan.

ADVANTAGES

GREATER TRAVEL DISTANCE

A vehicle allows you to travel further distances, faster. If your emergency bug out plan requires you to travel a far distance, then you should consider this option. However, this doesn't mean you have to choose a distant bug out location. You should always choose the best bug out location but not based on the distance.

MORE ROOM FOR SUPPLIES

A vehicle can easily carry more supplies and larger items than a person. When you have a good vehicle checklist as a part of your bug out plan, then you can turn your vehicle into a mobile bug out location. However, just because you can pack more supplies doesn't mean you should.

The goal is a good balance. Bring gear that will extend your independence and improve survival odds, but don't pack everything you can. Even if you pack supplies in your car, still have a BOB on hand in case something happens to your vehicle.

ADDITIONAL SHELTER OPTION

Even if you run out of gas or have other mechanical or electrical issues, a vehicle can provide shelter from rain and wind. If you can still run the vehicle, you can even have heating and cooling. A vehicle can give you shelter from a storm without having to set up a survival shelter or make any modifications. In a pinch, you can even use a hot engine to cook.

DISADVANTAGES

LEADS TO DEPENDENCE

Planning a good bug out vehicle is excellent, but you shouldn't consider this as the answer to all your survival problems. Plan your emergency bug out on the assumption that you may have to ditch your vehicle at some point. Running out of gas or an impassable road are just two possible incidents. Always plan on improvising rather than simply driving to your bug out location. Focus on honing survival skills and plan on having to get to your bug out destination on foot. The idea is always to think about the worst that can happen while hoping for the best to happen.

NOT AS VERSATILE

When you try to bug out, the road may be clogged with traffic or there might be a riot taking place on the road. In this case, do you think using a vehicle still the fastest way to bug out? What if something is cutting off a vital road to your destination? When you plan a bug out route consider whether or not going on foot is going to be a more direct means of travel since you can cut through terrain rather than have to stick to a specific road.

ADDED COMPLICATIONS

As we've shown above, traveling by vehicle can have some major advantages. However, even the best and most thought out bug out vehicle can potentially have added complications and can cost you more money. Consider the bug out vehicle addition as a whole when assessing what the best bug out vehicle is for your individual survival situation.

PLANNING THE BEST VEHICLE

The best bug out vehicle needs to have the following qualities to improve the advantages of a bug out vehicle while also minimizing the disadvantages.

4WD

This is obvious when picking out a bug out vehicle. It will vastly improve your options. A non-4WD car can break down if it needs to go off road. When your bug out vehicle has 4WD, then you can travel over more terrain and reach your bug out location faster.

MODULAR INTERIOR

Unless you are going to be bugging out in an RV, you should modify the interior of your vehicle to make it more tuned to survival. This means making room for more storage or convert it to sleeping quarters. While you want to improve and customize the interior as much as possible, you don't want to do anything to the engine or drivetrain.

If you customize in these areas, it will make repairs and part sourcing all the more difficult. When it comes to choosing a bug out vehicle, reliability is key and having stock parts make scavenging much easier.

DIESEL

Diesel engines have advantages over gas engines. For one, they are more fuel efficient. Second, they offer more fuel flexibility since you can also run them on heating oil, kerosene, and some jet fuels. This offers you greater scavenge potential while bugging out in an emergency. Diesel fuel also has a greater storage potential than gasoline. Due to commercially available fuel stabilizers, diesel fuel can last ten times longer than gasoline.

GAS MILEAGE

A bug out vehicle that gets low gas mileage is a sure way to run into problems. Gas is going to be in short supply after an emergency, and you may not have time to scavenge additional supplies while bugging out to your new location. Ideally, a vehicle should be rated at 23-27 MPG to get good enough gas efficiency during your evacuation.

EASY REPAIRS

When choosing the best bug out vehicle, the best thing to look for is reliability. You should be able to scavenge stock parts to do this. For this, you need to choose a vehicle that is widely used and has commonly available parts.

TRAILER HITCH

This opens up additional options for your bug out vehicle. You can include a trailer as a part of your bug out plan if needed. Trailers provide you with more cargo space without compromising passenger seating, which is great if you are bugging out in a group. You can also abandon a trailer as supplies get used up to improve gas mileage.

MANUAL TRANSMISSION

This isn't necessarily a requirement, but it can be beneficial. Manual transmission improves reliability, gas mileage and is easier to fix and replace than an automatic transmission. Manual transmissions also allow you to push start a car if you lose your keys or the ignition is burned out; improving your survival situation.

As you can see, there are a lot of options that can go into finding the best bug out vehicle. Knowing what works best for you is an important step in adding a vehicle to your bug out plan. Just remember not to depend on your bug out vehicle for survival. However, what if you don't have the money to buy a bug out vehicle? Let's look at how you can upgrade your current vehicle to make it survival ready.

7 WAYS TO UPGRADE YOUR VEHICLE FOR SURVIVAL

If you can't afford to buy a bug out vehicle then consider the following seven ways you can upgrade your vehicle and get it ready for a bug out situation.

1. UPGRADED TIRES

Your standard all-season tires won't work if you need to go off-road to get around traffic or blocked roads. You don't need monster truck tires; but you do need something that will keep you moving over mud, snow and loose gravel roads. Ideally, you should consider 31-33" tires, so you don't have to upgrade everything else around them or be unsafe on the road.

2. LOCKING DIFFERENTIAL

Without a locking differential, you may experience slippage when driving in mud and snow. A locking differential will keep the same power going to both wheels of that axle. This means that if one tire gets stuck in the mud, that other tire that is not in the mud will keep you going.

3. SUSPENSION LIFT

At the least, a decent suspension lift will give you greater ground clearance; which is great for running over rocks, debris, and other blockages. You only need about 2-3 inches of lift. Every inch of lift gives you about 3% more drag, which means you don't want to add too much lift otherwise it will hurt the fuel economy.

4. SKID PLATES

Since you're likely going to have to run a few things over with your new lifted suspension and tires, it is also a good idea to install skid plates over the important parts of your undercarriage. A good skid plate on the front guards the steering, front axle and bottom of the engine/oil pan. A mid-section plate is going to protect fuel lines, brake lines, and the passenger compartment. Rear plates will prevent your gas tank from getting damaged.

5. TRUCK SNORKEL

If you are going to be driving through water that is higher than the air intake for your engine, bad things are going to happen (has happened to me once). The engine will blow up if water gets inside it. Install a snorkel that will pull air from the same level as the roof of your vehicle, and you should be safe as long as your vehicle doesn't get totally submerged.

6. BRUSH GUARD

A brush guard is going to protect your front end and prevent things you hit from ruining your radiator. It will also protect your headlines and hood as well.

7. COMMUNICATIONS EQUIPMENT

In a survival situation, it is likely that cell phones and the internet won't work. Therefore, person-to-person communication is going to be the only way to keep in touch. The best place to start is with a high-quality CB radio. Mount one in your truck, and you'll be ready during an emergency. You may also want to consider installing a police scanner since it will be able to direct and navigate you away from bad situations.

Most survival upgrades, also work as standard off-road upgrades. This means you can simply look as if you are improving your truck and not preparing for a survival situation.

So now you are completely prepared with the proper gear and the planning stages of a disaster. But what do you do during an actual disaster and after such disaster? Let's take a look at these situations in the third and final book of these series.

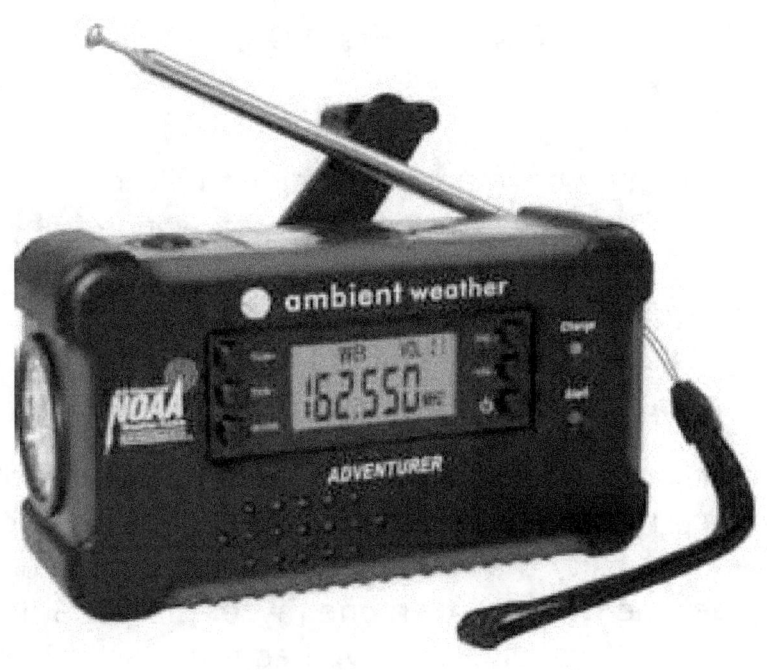

LAST WORDS

AS YOU may have noticed, I didn't talk much about firearms. Some of you may wonder why I didn't. Well, it is because most times firearms are not what give you the ultimate protection, but your survival skills and other gears do. Often firearms can cause more problems than they can actually solve.

But more importantly, I strongly believe only people should carry firearms that are well trained and know the responsibility that comes along with owning one. Don't get me wrong, I own one myself; it is a Smith & Wesson 629 revolver. I have had it for last 18 years, and I still frequent to a shooting range for practice.

Along with practice, it is important to learn the safekeeping and proper maintenance of a firearm are very to me, gun safety is very important, especially if you have children. This is one big reason my goal is to teach and train people to be self-reliant enough where they can face an epic disaster and survive without the help of a firearm.

The focus of these books are all about preparing for the ultimate disaster; I think it is best to learn various skills that you can use in real life to protect your family and provide food and shelter for them in an emergency.

Now, if you are a gun owner, I strongly urge you to protect the gun from your kids and make sure you get enough practice and know when and how to use it in a dire situation. Though using guns should always be your last resort, and knowing when to use it takes a lot of mental courage and steadiness. Remember, once the bullet has been fired from your gun, there is no turning back, and you have to live with the consequence.

So, if you do own a firearm, add that to your list of gears and make sure to have the gun fully protected and in safe and secure place and away from the children.

The last book in this series is the book all about what and how to live through an actual disaster and what and how to survive the aftermath of it. So it all about during and after scenarios of an actual disaster, while the last book and this book are all about the actual preparation process.

I wanted to thank you for buying my book; I am neither a professional writer nor an author, but rather a professional hiker and a bushcraft survival coach. I wanted to share my knowledge with you, as I know there are many people who share the same passion and drive as I do. So, this book is fully dedicated to you.

Despite my best effort to make this book error free, if you happen to find any errors, I want to ask for your forgiveness ahead of time.

Just remember, my writing skills may not be best, but the knowledge I share is pure and honest.

If you thought I added some value and shared some valuable information that you can use, please take a minute and post a review on wherever you bought this book from. This will mean the world to me. Thank you so much!!

Lastly, I wanted to thank Henry for his expert input throughout this book; he has been a great help, as he is considered the great expert in the field survival gear. Without him, this book would not have been possible.

If you need to get in touch with me for any reason, please feel free to email me at: BushcraftTrainer@gmail.com

Good Luck and Thank You!!!